The Architecture of Richard Rogers

Deyan Sudjic

The Architecture of Richard Rogers

Harry N. Abrams, Inc., Publishers

Library of Congress Catalog Card Number: 94-72680
ISBN 0-8109-1954-0

Copyright © 1994 Deyan Sudjic, Fourth Estate, and Wordsearch Ltd.

Published in 1995 by Harry N. Abrams, Incorporated, New York
A Times Mirror Company.
Printed and bound in Italy

Design: Gabriella Le Grazie
Editor: Caroline Roux

Photography (references are to page numbers)
AA Slide Library 34, 36, 37 top, 37 bottom, 39
Alex Bartel/Arcaid 60-1
Richard Bryant/Arcaid 42-3, 67, 68-9, 70, 71, 77
top left, top right, bottom, 78 top, bottom, 79,
88 top, 89 top right, top left, 92-3, 94 top left,
96 bottom right, bottom left, top, 104 top left,
bottom, 105 top left, top right, bottom
David Churchill/Arcaid 62
Peter Cook front cover, 52-3, 75 top left, bottom,
76, 82, 89 bottom, right, left, 94 left, right,
95, 100-1
Richard Davies 114-5, 119 bottom, 123
Richard Einzig/Arcaid 10,14 top, bottom, 18-19,
21 bottom, 23, 32-3, 41 top, middle, bottom,
42 top, 54, 56, 57, 58, 59, 62 bottom, 63
Ken Kirkwood 88, 97
John Linden 113 bottom
Eamon O'Mahony 27, 136, back cover
Paul Raftery/Arcaid 113 top
Masaki Sekiya 28, 104, 109
David Townend 12
Matthew Weinreb 94 top, 102, 103

Contents

1 | Design in a cold climate

The defining moment for British architecture of the early 1990s was the untimely death of James Stirling in 1992. It brought to an end an era that had begun when the servicemen came home from World War Two. People in their twenties who had fought in the war returned to take up their education where they had left off and filled the architecture schools. They brought with them a new determination and a new insight into the wider significance of what they were doing. The post-war period was marked initially by a profound belief in the social possibilities of architecture, then by disillusionment. In the case of Stirling, this led to a masterly new synthesis of conflicting architectural currents to produce a series of monumentally impressive buildings. But his sudden death left no obvious successor, although his practice continued under the leadership of his partner, Michael Wilford.

The sense of loss, both personal and professional, clearly marked Richard Rogers' face as he went on television on the evening of Stirling's death to pay tribute to his former tutor. He was barely able to keep his composure in front of the camera. It was a sad, poignant moment, yet the very fact that Stirling's death was considered important enough to merit so much airtime, and that it was Richard Rogers who was talking to a camera crew led by the controller of BBC2, Alan Yentob, said a great deal about the shifting public view of the relevance of architecture to Britain's wider cultural life. For the previous ten years Rogers and his one-time partner, Norman Foster, had been bracketed, rightly or wrongly, alongside Stirling as the personification of an unexpected architectural renaissance for Britain. The three were clearly very different architects, but they were all British, all enjoyed an impressive international reputation, and the careers of all three had been intertwined over several decades even if they belonged to different generations – Stirling was born in 1924, Rogers and Foster a decade later. Now the most senior and the most complex member of that trio had

Two buildings launched the career of both Richard Rogers and Norman Foster. Working together as Team Four, they built a house in Cornwall at Creek Vean, *left*, when they came back to Britain after studying in America, and then went on to design a factory for Reliance Controls in Swindon, *previous pages*. The spatial adventurousness of the house and the elegant structure of Reliance were qualities which both Rogers and Foster would develop further in their later work.

**Peter Rice the engineer,
above, whose brilliance
underpinned many of British
architecture's achievements,
left an unfillable void when
he died in 1993.**

gone. Stirling had a talent of genius, and its extinction left a huge gap. His inventiveness and belief in continuous experimentation had set the agenda for contemporary architecture in the widest sense, all around the world.

Rogers, approaching sixty, now had to face the prospect of his own mortality, and the realisation that he was no longer a youthful outsider but had metamorphosed into a leading figure of what passes for the architectural establishment. He had built his reputation as an iconoclast in his youth, but here he was, newly knighted and a well-regarded member of the great and the good: a former chairman of the trustees of the Tate Gallery; an adviser on architectural and planning issues to the Labour Party leadership; a Royal Academician; Chevalier de la Légion d'Honneur; and winner of institutional commissions to match. In Britain, where most architects are too inept or unworldly to understand the elementary rules of social conduct which allow them to take on such roles, these were real achievements. The European Court of Human Rights in Strasbourg, the headquarters of Channel 4 television, and Heathrow Airport's giant fifth terminal were all being designed by the Richard Rogers Partnership.

Yet with Stirling's death, there was nobody left from an older generation in Britain still active enough for Rogers to measure himself against, nobody to defer to, nobody to react against. If not quite Britain's architect laureate, since no such post actually existed, then Rogers was on the brink of the culminating stage of his career. In architecture, a profession in which youth has never been at a premium, this was no handicap. Indeed there are abundant examples from Louis Kahn onwards of architects who have only begun to build at all past the age of fifty.

The death of the highly gifted engineer Peter Rice in 1993 had a different, but perhaps even more troubling, significance for Rogers. For twenty years, he had relied on Rice's incisive brilliance, from the design of the Pompidou Centre onwards, not merely to solve problems, but also as a source of inspiration in his search for creative excellence. Rice offered insights into ways of doing things rather than ready-made solutions. He was as much a creative designer as any architect, and in the climate in which Rogers was working, where historical, symbolic or decorative alibis cut very little ice, Rice's philosophical insights into the nature of materials and structure offered the kind of resonance that architecture limited by pragmatic functionalism seemed increasingly to lack. Rice's enthusiasm for exploring naturally occurring structural patterns and learning from them was a substitute for classical aesthetic theory. He had worked on the Sydney Opera House, and gone on to become involved with many of the most challenging structural engineering designs of the next three decades. Without his input, little of what has come to be known as the English High-Tech School – the work of the group that includes Rogers, Foster, Nicholas Grimshaw, Michael Hopkins, Future Systems and Ian Ritchie – would have achieved such a level of refinement.

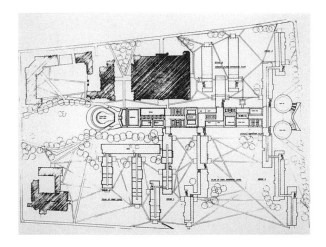

Rogers and Foster worked together as post-graduate students at Yale, collaborating on a scheme for an academic megastructure, *above and below*. The division between served and servant spaces, with clearly expressed service towers providing a sense of order to the whole, derives from the ideas of Louis Kahn – and suggests the direction that Rogers' work in particular was to follow.

Rogers found himself at a watershed in the shifting landscape of contemporary architecture. His career up to this point had been shaped by just two, albeit overwhelmingly powerful, buildings: the Centre Georges Pompidou in Paris, that he had begun work on with Renzo Piano in 1971, and the equally startling Lloyd's of London building, completed in 1986. Now it was changing gear. There were, of course, many other buildings both large and small that Rogers and his partners had designed and built in the intervening years, from the flamboyant technological expressionism of the Inmos microprocessor factory at Newport in Wales, to the deft conversion of Billingsgate, London's Victorian fishmarket, into modern dealing room space. There was the famous slate and blockwork Team 4 house, slipped delicately into the Cornish landscape, that had started it all in the 1960s, and the vivid GRC-skinned UOP factory outside London from the 1970s. Each had its own qualities, and each would doubtless have had more individual critical attention were it not for the overwhelming impact of the Pompidou and Lloyd's.

These two buildings transformed Rogers from a talented architect of local significance into a world figure. They gave his work a rhetorical content and, being built at a time when the optimistic modernism that inspired them was itself under threat, they were inevitably read as a powerful reassertion of the relevance of the architectural avant-garde. Yet even without them, Rogers' career would have had a distinctive trajectory, marked by his hedonistic enthusiasm for the modern world.

Richard Rogers was born in Florence in 1933 of cultured, comfortable professional Anglo-Italian parents, the first of two sons. For the first six years of his life he was brought up as an Italian, with the family only moving to Britain just before the outbreak of World War Two to find themselves virtual foreigners, despite their British passports. Those early years left their mark and Florence even now remains a

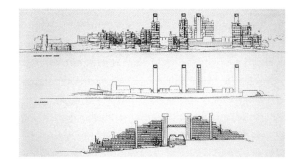

With its turf roof and contour-hugging cross-section, the house in Creek Vean, *above*, brought to Cornwall some of the informality and sense of connection with the natural setting that Rogers had seen in America. Technically, the daring use of glass set directly into blockwork was a new departure for Britain.

powerful architectural memory – for the ferment of innovation and experiment that characterised the early renaissance whose traces were all around him, from Brunelleschi's dome for the Duomo (the first attempted in the west since Roman times) to the expressive quality of the Foundling Hospital; and for the vocabulary of classicism with which the city is inevitably associated. As a result, his sensibility has always been that of a European, rather than more narrowly focused on a specifically British perspective. Meanwhile his parents – his father was a doctor, and his mother an enthusiastic potter – played an important role, instilling in their children a commitment to modern culture in all its forms, from art to science to psychoanalysis. England, however, and in particular its boarding school educational system, was a rude shock after Italy. Small wonder that Rogers turned out to be dyslexic, and a fragile, vulnerable personality in his school years.

Yet in the Britain of the early 1950s, as he emerged from military service that ironically took him back to Italy to begin his studies, Rogers cut an exotic figure. His architectural education was a catholic one and placed him within the tradition of modernism in a European context. His first halting drawings as a teenager were made in the studio of his famous uncle Ernesto Rogers in the Milanese partnership BBPR. Rogers later graduated from the Architectural Association in 1959, the year after Peter Cook and the other members of what was to become Archigram arrived there as students. He was thus directly engaged both with an older generation of Italians who had been keen to remake the architecture of the pioneers in a more lyrical way, and with an excitable group of youthful upstarts for whom only the most extreme definitions of architecture were supportable.

At this time, the Architectural Association was at the peak of its prestige as one of the world's leading schools of architecture. Alan Colquhoun, Peter Smithson and James Gowan were among its many distinguished teachers, as was James Stirling. Rogers also remembers Robert Furneaux Jordan and John Killick as other teachers who helped to shape his student years. Rogers' career there was chequered: he showed little aptitude for drawing, but he had the academic potential to collect a clutch of scholarships that took him to the United States for post-graduate study. Looking across the Atlantic was to prove a liberating experience for many of his generation, not least for Rogers. He went to America with Su Brumwell, whom he had just married, and the American introductions that her family were able to make through the sculptor Naum Gabo, in whose house they lived at Yale, allowed them to meet Alexander Calder, as well as the critic Lewis Mumford. It was also at Yale that Rogers met Foster, and where both of them were taught for a while by James Stirling as a visiting critic.

America gave Rogers a taste for the work of Louis Kahn and Frank Lloyd Wright, and an insight into the visual power and vigour of American architecture, in contrast to the

Reliance Controls, *below*, showed the emergence of what were to become the guiding principles of the Pompidou: a legible vocabulary of components with clear distinctions between steel beams in compression and the diagonal tension bracing rods.

intellectual traditions of the Europeans. But the biggest revelation for the British in America in the late 1950s was California. They found it was not, as they had been indoctrinated to believe at home, the embodiment of superficial vulgarity, but a place of possibilities and experimentation. The Case Study Houses – the remarkable initiative to build innovative new light-weight housing around Los Angeles organised in the 1950s by John Entenza of the magazine *Art and Architecture* – were to become a pilgrimage centre for architects of Rogers' generation. Craig Ellwood, a leading member of the new Californian architectural scene, was a visiting professor at Yale in 1960. He met Stirling there, and persuaded him to make his first trip to the West Coast. Stirling returned from California with a collection of images of what was, at the time, little-known recent work, and took them back to London. Rogers went to see for himself. Charles Eames' and Raphael Soriano's designs left a particular impression, as did the underlying premise: the use of industrial components and prefabrication to build housing that was not only economical and potentially capable of being built in high volume, but which was also beautiful.

At Yale, Foster and Rogers worked together on their student projects, under the direction of Serge Chermayeff – the Russian-born emigré who had moved to America by way of London and a spell in partnership with Erich Mendelsohn. They were taught by Paul Rudolph, too, and influenced by the more distant presence of Louis Kahn. Rogers talked and looked, Foster drew.

It was also at Yale that Rogers completed the third of three pieces of writing that marked the critical stages in his architectural education. At the Architectural Association, he had written an extended essay on planning and utopia – which was failed by Peter Smithson, and subsequently passed by the school's principal. Another essay looked at the Maison de Verre built by the decorator and interior designer Pierre

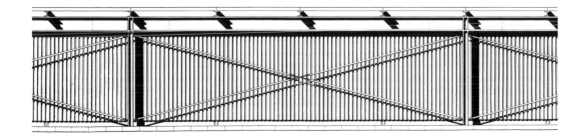

Chareau for Doctor Dalsace in Paris in the 1930s; it was published by *Domus* magazine in 1966. In the essay, Rogers describes the Maison de Verre as 'a unique masterpiece'. While 'Le Corbusier's buildings are conceived as an active play of mass and solids, and are monumental in form, the Chareau house consists of a free-standing skeleton structure enclosed by an active skin, with non-static screens poised in space.' Rogers' American dissertation was on the Californian work of Rudolph Schindler. While the impact of Rogers' continuing enthusiasm for Shindler is not so immediately apparent as is his fascination with the Maison de Verre, it is genuine.

After graduation, Rogers drove across America. He worked briefly for SOM, then went back to Britain with Su to set up in practice with Foster and his wife, Wendy Cheeseman, as Team 4. A highly self-conscious choice of name, Team 4 hints not just at the famous Team X group organised by Alison and Peter Smithson, Aldo Van Eyck and Giancarlo de Carlo, but is also an attempt to deny the cult of personality, and asserts the idea of the designer not as a heroic formgiver, but as a disinterested professional working co-operatively with others engaged in a scientific endeavour. And indeed, Rogers had acquired a genuine sense of the kind of social mission that had underpinned an important strand in the modernism of the 1920s. In Rogers' case however, it was filtered through the influences of student life. He was in America before the anti-Vietnam War demonstrations but in time for the Freedom marches, and experienced at first hand the emergence of the so-called counter culture. It left a profound impression, both personally and on his work. The very idea of professionalism was under attack, a concept that was played down in favour of advocacy. The politically correct way for the architect to work was not to impose professional solutions, but to find the real clients and involve them in the process of design. In the case of housing, that meant answering not to the developer or the housing bureaucracy, but to the residents. It was a deeply problematic but well-meaning approach. Architecture was beginning to be seen not as concerned with the creation of individual monuments, but as a means to provide solutions to the perennial problems facing much of mankind in the provision of even the most elementary forms of shelter. Rogers had a pretty firm idea of himself in that he had no intention of turning into a conventional, corporate professional. He had begun to see architecture as linked with the wider world of the arts; the spatial vision of the constructivists, for example, had moved him considerably. But architecture was also, as far as he was concerned, a social mission. The difference between the sense of moral certainty of the pioneering modernists, with their belief in the rightness of functionalism, and the attitudes of the 1960s was the conception that the architect now had to accept a sense of responsibility in his use of scarce resources and energy, and put them to work to appropriate ends.

Ostensibly designed to reflect a non-hierarchical, modern workplace, and with the flexibility to accommodate future change, Reliance Controls, *opposite*, was eventually demolished less than 25 years after it was built, the victim of a rate of technological change even more rapid than its forward-looking architects had expected.

A retaining wall forms the backdrop for the gallery space at the back of the Creek Vean house, *previous pages.* **As a building type it could not be further removed from the projects that the Rogers office was working on in Tokyo thirty years later,** *above.* **But both demonstrate a concern with innovation as well as form. In Cornwall Team 4 experimented with new glazing techniques. In Tokyo the Richard Rogers Partnership tried to use the form of the building to generate wind power.**

Notwithstanding their ambitions, Team 4's first project of note was that most traditional of commissions for young architects embarking on a new career through the ages: a house for a relative. They were asked to design a home in Cornwall for Marcus and Rene Brumwell, and their art collection. Marcus Brumwell, Rogers' father-in-law, was a founder member of the pioneering design consultancy Design Research Unit, as well as the director of an advertising agency. He had close personal connections with the cultural elite of the 1930s and 1940s, from Ben Nicholson to Bernard Leach. He was involved with Mass Observation and the Labour Party. In his days in advertising he had commissioned many of the leading graphic artists, and he took the house as an opportunity to extend his patronage into architecture with an equally acute eye. To fund the house, Brumwell sold a Mondrian painting he had acquired as an act of generosity during the war when the Dutch artist, then almost unknown in Britain, was living penniless in London.

Creek Vean is an architectural *tour de force* which exploits to the full a magnificent coastal position, perched on the edge of a narrow wooded creek overlooking the Fal estuary. It is half buried into the contours of the site and offers a spatial complexity and informality that seems closer to California than Cornwall. Living and dining rooms are contained in a compact double-volume block while a longer, lower wing houses bedrooms and top-lit gallery space. The building frames a series of spectacular views looking out over the waters of the creek below, culminating in a two-storey all-glass south-facing wall. The house has a spatial fluidity as well as demonstrating a confident synthesis of formal invention with ingenious detailed design. There are few signs of the later preoccupation of both Foster and Rogers with lightweight, prefabricated buildings, indeed the materials have a monumentality and permanence to them that might almost have something to do with the houses designed by Wright that they had seen in America. Floors are slate, and the same untreated blockwork is used inside and out for walls and partitions, and to create bookshelves and worktops. Only the entrance bridge, spanning a steep gully between the road and a turfed roof, has in its form a suggestion of the direction their later work was to take. However, Creek Vean was technically inventive; its full-height glazing is held in place with neoprene gaskets, one of the very first uses of this technique in Britain. And in planning terms, the open-ended quality of the rooms, designed for easy extension, also displayed the preoccupations of the young practice.

Team 4 designed several other houses, worked on planning studies for larger housing developments, and entered a number of competitions. The houses were distinguished by open, informal plans, and an interest in exploiting changes of level and energetic cross-sections to embrace their natural settings as closely as possible. But the project which attracted the most attention for the practice during its brief existence

Jan Kaplicky's montage, *above*, showed the essential principle of the first Rogers office in London, completed in 1971 – a lightweight metal skin structure below, attached to the top of an existing traditionally built block. The studio, *below*, was a frank reflection of the construction methods.

was a new factory for Reliance Controls on the outskirts of Swindon, completed in 1967 just before the partnership was dissolved. At the time, the factory – which was demolished twenty years later – received far more coverage than the Cornwall house partly, perhaps, because the young Team 4 was a little uncomfortable with the idea of being identified with designing comfortable seaside homes. Rogers saw himself as a radical, agonised about homelessness, and enthusiastically espoused the cause of industrialised building in an attempt to deal with it. Against this background, Reliance Controls – the picture, if not the substance, of the modern workplace – seemed a more appropriate building to identify with, and indeed was a much more effective calling card in the struggle to find the all-important next job. Certainly Reliance, which came closer to Charles Eames or Craig Ellwood in its spirit than to Mies van der Rohe, was a handsome structure, which seemed to be a world away from the crude banality of the English industrial estate. Like Ellwood's work, it uses an elegant painted steel structure. And in a clear tribute to Alison and Peter Smithson's Hunstanton School, the only post-war British work before Stirling and Gowan's Leicester University building to secure the undivided admiration of Rogers and his peers, it makes a monumental campanile out of its water tank, raised up on four steel I beams.

In the allegedly classless 1960s, Team 4 also made much of the supposedly democratic nature of the building: 'a single entrance is provided for all staff', they announced proudly. That might not seem like much now, but in the 'Us and Them' days of three decades ago, it was at least a step in the right direction. In retrospect, however, the building looks a little insubstantial set beside the sustained invention and the spatial richness of the Creek Vean house. In the end, its relevance to Rogers' career is in its development of a carefully organised and considered hierarchy of structure, bracing and cladding, put together with a legibility and elegance that may

To a remarkable degree the Pompidou Centre as built, *opposite*, faithfully reflected the spirit of the original competition drawings, *above*. Not only did the finished building have the striking exposed structure originally envisaged, but more importantly it became exactly the kind of social catalyst that its architects had envisaged.

be compared to the diagonally braced structural bays at the Pompidou.

For Rogers, one of the most important elements of Reliance Controls was the way in which its exterior clearly expressed the role of each component. To the architecturally initiated at least, the diagonal cross-bracing rods were obviously in tension, keeping the structure rigid against the tendency of wind loading to deform it, while the much deeper I beams were in compression, carrying the majority of the load, and the profiled sheet metal was visibly no more than a cladding infill. It was at this point in his career that Rogers became aware of his interest in searching for an approach to architecture that could accept some level of improvisation and change within the clarity of its structural framework, which he saw as marking a divergence between his own work and that of Norman Foster. Rogers, along with Eames and Archigram, was interested in the idea of coping with visible change. Foster's work belonged, in Rogers' eyes at least, to another tradition which Foster shared with Mies van der Rohe, that of formal perfection which is finite and closed.

From very early on Rogers had fretted over the limitations of the building industry and its refusal to accept even the most primitive technological innovations. Working on one housing project in Team 4 days, Rogers discovered to his horror that the waterproof membrane he had specified in his drawings was being interpreted in the form of a layer of bitumen-soaked newspapers. The experience left a lasting mark on him, instilling in the architect the determination to design buildings which minimised their dependence on the haphazard accidents of conventional building-site methods, and were based instead on prefabrication where production lines and quality control could iron out the wet, muddy chaos of open-air site conditions. Rather than glueing bricks together with wet mortar, or pouring concrete into hand-made wooden moulds much as the Romans had done, Rogers unquestioningly accepted the dream of a technologically-based architecture. The dream saw prefabricated building components being helicoptered into place from automated factories, ready to be snapped together in the course of a few days, not months. Building skins could be as technologically sophisticated as the monocoque structure of aircraft wings. And buildings themselves could become machines: light, responsive and adaptable. From Le Corbusier's conception of the house as, metaphorically at least, a machine for living in, to Jean Prouvé's attempts to design buildings that were literally mechanical, in which not only the walls but the floors too could be reconfigured at will, this was a dream that had been around since the nineteenth century in one way or another.

Joseph Paxton, the master of prefabrication and air-conditioning, more engineer than architect, was the hero of Victorian architecture as far as Rogers was concerned, and not Waterhouse or Butterfield. Paxton's Crystal Palace may have been condemned as ugly at the time, but it was a building that stunned the public and caught the

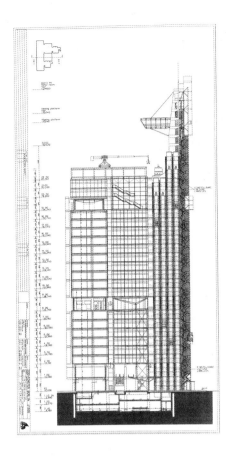

By the 1990s the Richard Rogers Partnership was working around the world: in Germany, with this tower for Berlin, *above*; on a masterplan for a new business district in Shanghai, *opposite*; and in Korea, Japan, France and the Czech republic. The global spread of the office's workload marked the increasing preoccupation of the partnership with environmentally responsible design, and with new approaches to urbanism.

imagination of progressive-minded engineers and architects around the world. It redefined architecture in a way that cut across the traditional conception of permanent and massive masonry, and replaced it with a vision of light-weight high-performance buildings that seemed far more relevant to Rogers than any of the more conventional Victorian designers. Reyner Banham's influential book, *The Architecture of the Well-Tempered Environment,* published in 1969, summed up a view of architecture as no more than a question of environmental manipulation, which vividly expressed Rogers' attitudes at the time. 'One must observe a fundamental difference between environmental aids of the structural type, and those of which the campfire is the archetype. Let the difference be expressed in a form of parable in which a savage tribe arrives at an evening camp site and finds it well supplied with fallen timber. Two basic methods of exploiting the environmental potential of that timber exist: either it may be used to construct a wind-break, or a rain-shed – the structural solution; or it may be used to build a fire – the power-operated solution. An ideal tribe of noble rationalists would consider the amount of wood available, and make an estimate of the probable weather for the night – wet, windy, or cold – and dispose of its timber resources accordingly.' A real tribe, Banham noted acidly, being the inheritors of ancestral cultural predispositions, 'would do nothing of the sort, of course, and would either make fire, or build shelter according to prescribed custom.'

Rogers belonged to a generation of architects who were eager to free themselves from those prescribed tribal customs, to treat architecture instead as a matter of systems and possibilities, rather than archetypes. He admired the Maison de Verre because, 'each element had been conceived in the light of its function, with the mind of an inventor, rather than by an organiser of existing knowledge'. Machines themselves were also changing. In the pioneering days of the Bauhaus they were titanic and threatening, pumping out steam, and clanking and whirring. By the 1960s they could be sleek and seductive or even playful. And it was this incarnation of the machine that was to prove so important for Rogers' buildings conceived in that brief interlude of the transistor era that slipped in between the turbine epoch and the age of the microprocessor, when moving parts gave way to anorexic plastic and beeps. Equally important, when Rogers reached maturity technology was not yet regarded as an entirely negative force. The world was still deeply impressed by the image of power and achievement represented by the vast rockets of the American space programme, and the structures of Cape Canaveral. Technology, if put to use for the right ends, seemed capable of solving any problem, no matter how complex.

With the dissolution of Team 4 in 1967, Richard and Su Rogers set up in practice on their own, with John Young joining them as a partner. Eventually they moved into an extension on top of the DRU building in Aybrook Street, London that they designed and which was instantly dubbed the Yellow Submarine. In fact, the most telling image of the building, the montage produced by Jan Kaplicky who was the project architect for the structure, was automotive rather than nautical in its inspiration. It shows a Volkswagen Beetle car on top of an undistinguished industrial structure, connected to it by an umbilical cord of flexible pipes and hoses. Aluminium windows like windscreens are riveted into three-metre wide aluminium cladding panels as bulbous as car body panels. The implication is that the structure is not only delivered ready-made to the site, but can also be unplugged and moved on when conditions change. Nothing of the kind happened, and the structure is there today, long after Rogers moved his office, though it is now a faded beige colour rather than the original vibrant yellow.

In 1971 Rogers established a new partnership with Renzo Piano, an architect from Genoa who shared his taste for radical applications of technology and, as they both saw it, its liberating potential. 'Technology is not an end in itself but must aim at solving long-term social and ecological problems,' wrote Rogers. And Piano remembers, 'We came together at a time when we had built some things separately, but in a spirit that was close enough; some houses, factories and offices in England and Italy. We were both looking to escape academicism, to connect with a certain artisanal tradition in architecture, and above all to use the most contemporary

techniques. If we were inexperienced for architects of thirty-three and thirty-five, we had a certain freshness, a naivety that would serve us well in what was to come.'

Almost by accident Piano and Rogers entered the international competition organised by the French government for the design of a cultural centre in Paris to cover one million square feet on a car park site in the Les Halles area. The rest is history. Rogers has subsequently admitted to having been persuaded to enter the competition against his better instincts. He saw no prospect of producing a building that would be anything other than a monument to the highly centralised and autocratic French presidential system. In the event Piano and Rogers' entry, selected by a jury that included their hero Jean Prouvé as well as Philip Johnson and Oscar Niemeyer, was a literally fantastic fusion of the seductive but unbuildable imagery of Archigram and Victorian engineering that combined visual bravura with structural pragmatism. Underpinning their approach was a passionate conviction that the traditional didactic museum was no longer appropriate in the modern world. In its place Piano and Rogers envisaged a high-tech agora, a special place within the city that would be part of the public domain; a substitute setting for the life driven off the streets by zoning and motor traffic.

Without being entirely clear how it could be realised, Piano and Rogers proposed a structure designed by Ted Happold and Peter Rice of Ove Arup and Partners, that was more a flexible framework than a traditional building and had a clearly acknowledged debt to both Archigram and Cedric Price's Fun Palace project of 1961. 'Ted Happold encouraged us to enter,' remembers Piano, 'but we hesitated. It really took us two or three weeks to make up our minds. We had work, not much, but enough to occupy us, and we had never faced a cultural brief before.' But enter they did, and in their submission Piano and Rogers wrote: 'It is our belief that buildings should be able to change, not only in plan, but in section and elevation, allowing people freedom to do their own things, the order and scale and grain coming from a clear understanding and expression of the process of building, and the optimisation of each individual element, its system, of manufacture, storage, transportation, erection and connection, all within a clearly defined and rational framework. This framework must allow people to perform freely inside and out, to change and adapt, in answer to technical or client needs, this free and changing performance becoming an expression of the architecture of the building – a giant Meccano set rather than a traditional static transparent or solid doll's house. Exciting things happen when a variety of overlapping activities designed for all people, the old and the young, the blue and white collar workers, locals and visitors all meet, opening up the possibility of interaction outside institutional limits. When this takes place, deprived areas become dynamic places where all can participate, rather than less or more beautiful ghettoes'. These were concepts that underpinned both the Pompidou Centre and the Lloyd's building, designed after

Offices for Lloyd's Register of Shipping, *above,* **on a sensitive semi-rural site in Hampshire, were designed to make the most of passive energy saving as well as the natural context. The project is in the grounds of a freestanding Victorian villa, an image which helped to define the architectural approach to the new building.**

another competition when Piano and Rogers finally agreed to part professionally. Lloyd's pushed that particular path of architectural inquiry to its logical conclusion, and it left Rogers searching for new challenges.

At the start of the 1990s, the structure of the Rogers office was changing too, and so was its workload. The commissions continued to come in, with a weight and variety that matched the partnership's international reputation. Yet none of them seemed to offer quite the same possibilities for making an impact that his two landmark buildings had done. Perhaps it was because Rogers had already proved his point. Designing buildings that were consciously of the present rather than being bogged down in over self-conscious historical references no longer seemed so outlandish as it once had. The challenge of post-modernism had passed. The Pompidou had been a triumphant reassertion of the power of unrestrained inventiveness. Lloyd's was an astonishing sleight of hand – a building that could only be called extreme had been smuggled into the heart of a city that was, at least in architectural terms, the most culturally conservative in Europe. And despite the initial chorus of protest from conservationists, and later the tarnishing of the reputation of the institution that had built it, the Lloyd's building has been assimilated into Londoners' mental geography of their city with surprising speed as an essential, even popular, element of the skyline.

Rogers had moved on from designing buildings whose success or failure represented a battle between opposing architectural movements, into a position to design buildings that stood or fell primarily on their intrinsic merits. These buildings were concerned no longer with making momentous statements about the philosophy of design, but were about more pragmatic concerns: about making offices that were good places in which to work; about devising functional but aesthetically convincing factories and studios; about helping to make cities better places in which to live; and about using energy and

resources responsibly and sparingly. The Richard Rogers Partnership had translated itself from a highly focused studio dedicated to producing astonishingly complex one-off buildings virtually one at a time, into an international consultancy with sixty employees and four partners. John Young, Marco Goldschmied and Mike Davies have worked with Rogers for more than twenty years. Each of the partners brings a different range of skills to the practice and ensures that it is more than a vehicle for Rogers alone, a transition which brings up the great undiscussed subject of architectural authorship.

The clearer it becomes that making a building is no more a one-man affair than making a feature film, the more that the world insists on regarding it as an act of lonely individual creation. Architectural practice has become polarised between the high-profile signature architect on the one hand and commodity design on the other, where design is offered as part of a building package with other services and the client's primary interest is in minimising cost. The non-stars who still attempt to offer a traditional architectural service are being squeezed out between these two poles. The signature architect is increasingly treated as an artist. Certain clients commission the Richard Rogers Partnership for a Richard Rogers building, just as they might install a Henry Moore or a Richard Serra outside their corporate headquarters, and hang a Schnabel or a Warhol in the board room. The choice of architect makes a statement about the taste, status and ambition of the client, and as such it is a given that the work will carry the recognisable signature of the architect or the artist. Rogers and Foster, just as much as Richard Meier or Michael Graves, have become architectural brands. This can mean that the architect's office exists only to serve the founder as a vehicle staffed by subservient designers skilled at interpreting and echoing the founder's style, or it can give other talents the chance to have a major input in the direction of the office at a stage in their careers when they would not have a chance to

The first to be completed of a series of Tokyo buildings designed by the Richard Rogers Partnership was this mixed office and commercial structure at Kabuki-cho in Tokyo, *left.* **The form reflects the intricacies of Japanese zoning laws; the steel work was fabricated in the UK and shipped to Japan.**

Building Heathrow Airport's giant new fifth terminal, *opposite*, will keep the practice busy into the early years of the next century.

work on high-profile commissions under their own names. In Rogers' case, the direction of the office's work has been shaped by self-selection. Those architects who want to work for Rogers are there because they want to work on the kind of buildings that he designs. There is no ambiguity about it. Yet they are not plain and simple Rogers buildings. It would have been impossible for him to have built Lloyd's without John Young's single-minded commitment to innovation in detail and material, Marco Goldschmied's sense of reality, Mike Davies' passion for lyrical technological imagery, or Laurie Abbott's remarkable gift for deftly conjuring up ideas in graphic form.

If the battle for modernism was over, the Richard Rogers Partnership was in the position to find new areas to make its own. The question of urbanism is now a major one, and the ecological characteristics of new developments is another. These are the issues which have preoccupied its work in the 1990s. Meanwhile, the scale and ambition of the urban projects tackled by the firm have become steadily larger, culminating in a project for the mayor of Shanghai to define a masterplan for a new business district for the city to contain upwards of 20 million square feet of accommodation. There have been commissions for the centre of Berlin, for the docklands in Liverpool and for urban development in France. At the same time, the office has become increasingly preoccupied with notions of sustainability and appropriateness. Its city plans attempt to create communities based on public transport; its individual buildings attempt to do without air-conditioning wherever possible. In stylistic terms, the definition of a Rogers building has become wider and wider. It can be the Mendelsohn-influenced law courts in Strasbourg, the sweeping curves of the new Terminal Five at Heathrow, or the sleek sculptural forms of the latest designs for the Tomigaya wind turbine tower in Tokyo. With its work in the Far East, such as the prefabricated housing in Korea, and in Eastern Europe, where the firm is working with Future Systems on proposals for a science park in the Czech republic, and its offices in Berlin and Tokyo, the partnership has become a truly modern architectural practice.

Not all of Rogers' designs have been translated into buildings. Some of the partnership's most striking projects – such as the European headquarters for the Japanese bank Daiwa in London, or the Tokyo Forum project – have not been realised. But the drawings have been almost as influential as completed buildings. Through almost thirty years of practice, Rogers has remained faithful to his basic principals, while continually refining, modifying and updating his work. If you compare the Lloyd's building to the new Channel 4 headquarters, for example, you see two designs that rely on the refinement of their detail, and the elegance with which their structure is expressed in their form. But, like successive motor car models or new generations of computers, each achieve that in very different ways.

2 A modern practice

When Richard Rogers went to the Architectural Association as a student in the early 1950s, Britain's major contribution to the development of contemporary architectural discourse was the new town – an undeniable achievement in terms of organisation and vision, but questionable in terms of its intrinsic design quality. In its establishment of the Welfare State, Britain had also initiated a building programme for a new generation of schools that was the envy of the world, and attracted constant streams of pilgrims eager to see the results. But apart from the schools and housing, the most conspicuous new pieces of architecture were Frederick Gibberd's first terminal for Heathrow Airport, the LCC's Festival Hall and Basil Spence's Coventry Cathedral, buildings of no more than purely local significance. Architectural culture in Britain was dominated by the art historical scholarship of Nikolaus Pevsner, while practitioners still laboured under the shadow of the Festival of Britain, an event whose architectural content the more daring members of the younger generation had regarded with ill-concealed disgust, viewing it as impossibly tainted by saccharine-sweet sentimentality despite its popular success.

The country's architecture was perceived by younger professionals as limply provincial, poised at the sentimental end of one of its periodic oscillations between compromise and bloodyminded inventiveness. The avant-garde, if there actually was one, was represented by the Independent Group, a circle that included the critic Reyner Banham, Alison and Peter Smithson, and certain of the putative parents of Pop Art such as Eduardo Paolozzi and Richard Hamilton. The Smithsons believed in toughness, professing to be more interested in sociology than in developing harmonic proportional systems based on classical precedents for the façades of their buildings. Their Hunstanton School, finally completed in 1954, and the Economist building of 1964 represented the high watermark of this tendency, which came to be known as the New

For Rogers' generation of students, Alison and Peter Smithson represented the highpoint of the British architectural avant-garde. Their Economist building in London, *left*, was completed in 1964. A suave and sophisticated tower, it was seen as a sharp riposte to the shallow charm of Gibberd, Spence and the Festival of Britain.

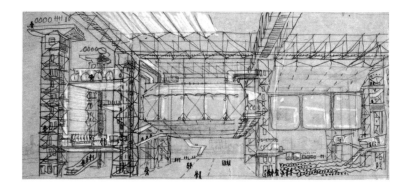

Richard Rogers | A modern practice

Cedric Price's Fun Palace project of 1961, *above*, clearly planted ideas in Piano's and Rogers' minds. The exposed steel framework, offering the flexible accommodation, and the name itself were a starting point for their design for the Pompidou Centre. Pierre Chareau's 1928 Maison de Verre, *opposite page, top*, influenced all the high-tech school. But for Rogers in particular it was a revelation. Provocative designs from Archigram, such as Ron Herron's Walking City of 1964, *opposite*, also helped to pave the way for the Pompidou.

Brutalism. It was a movement that deliberately set out to present itself as a self-consciously prickly antidote to the sickly Scandinavian charm of Festival of Britain style by making a virtue out of the blunt directness with which materials were put together. The Smithsons also stood out for their determination to create an intellectual climate for architecture and to see themselves as part of an international process. They were involved in Team X, and its part in the collapse of the CIAM and the demise of the older generation of modernists.

While its industrial and financial leadership in the nineteenth century had made Victorian Britain a dynamic driving force for architecture, the twentieth century had seen British architecture marginalised. Charles Rennie Mackintosh had enjoyed an enormous international reputation before the First World War, but found it impossible to make a living as an architect in the 1920s and took to producing watercolours instead. Lutyens, at the other end of the spectrum, had yet to be critically rehabilitated. In the 1950s nobody talked about him other than, as Robert Furneaux Jordan put it in his dismissive assessment of nineteenth-century revivalists, *Victorian Architecture* (Harmondsworth 1966), in terms of being a talent clean out of time. Since the 1920s, architecture in Britain had declined into isolated complacency, or into a pale provincial echo of more determined and vigorous movements elsewhere. Nothing attempted in the 1950s came anywhere near matching the achievement of the Crystal Palace, the focus of the Great Exhibition of 1851.

Sporadic attempts had been made to import the continental version of modernism into Britain before the war, and the best of them are to be seen in such direct transplants as Mendelsohn and Chermayeff's flat-roofed, white-walled house in Old Church Street, Chelsea – a composition with all Mendelsohn's trademark motifs, including curved glass stair towers. (Ironically it is being remodelled in the 1990s by Norman Foster, to the vocal opposition of a new generation of heritage lobbyists – the sort who would undoubtedly have attacked the building of the structure in the first place.) Gropius managed to build a not particularly distinguished school near Cambridge, while Lubetkin and Tecton's flats in Highgate attracted the admiration of Le Corbusier himself.

This purist architectural strand underpinned the start of the career of Denys Lasdun, who went on to design the brutalist National Theatre on London's South Bank in the 1970s. In the 1930s he had designed an accomplished neo-Corbusian house and worked as a member of Tecton. However, most of the Modern Movement-influenced design in Britain at the time was no more than an adoption of superficially fashionable mannerisms. Sweden was more often a model – as can be seen in a string of progressive brick town halls from Norwich to Hornsey – than France, Germany, or even Holland. The legacy of Lutyens was more influential for a significant number

of architects than the impact of the Bauhaus. And Lutyens was followed by such sternly traditionalist practitioners as Albert Richardson, who continued to build historical revivalism right into the 1950s .

There was a strong and persistent current of conservatism in the English scene. In the 1930s the great and the good of Hampstead had done their best to stop Erno Goldfinger, the Hungarian emigré who had worked for August Perret in Paris, from building a modest enough little row of houses in the area. There was a recurring undercurrent of chauvinistic opposition to the importation of what were described as alien architectural attitudes. Throughout that decade, its critics took to describing the International Style as 'modernismus', evoking a sinister conflation of cultural threats part-Teutonic, part-Bolshevik. Given this background, it was predictable that the most successful argument raised in Goldfinger's defence was the notion that his austere flat-roofed brick elevations represented nothing more threatening than an update of the Georgian vernacular. Basil Spence, perhaps the principal ornament of British architecture in the 1950s, based his career on an attempt to straddle the opposing poles of conservatism and radicalism. Having worked in Lutyens' office, he subsequently did his best to synthesise formal planning with Le Corbusier, veering from Coventry Cathedral to Sussex University, from neo-Gothic to neo-Modern.

If the hold of the Modern Movement on Britain was feeble to begin with, the effect of its hijacking by the post-war developers as the style of choice for town centre redevelopments proved nearly fatal. As has been endlessly recounted, it provided the philosophical justification for a tabula rasa approach to the redevelopment of its towns and cities. Actually it was more hit-and-run than free plan. Banal, simplistic designs –

driven by cynical cost-cutting rather than aesthetic principle – gave modernism an almost terminally bad name, and contributed significantly to a climate of disillusionment. Both the conservatives and the radicals began to question the inadequacies of the Modern Movement's legacy. For some the solution was to go back to traditional forms that were at least technically proven, and to return to the picturesque ideal of the city that has its roots in Camillo Sitte's writings on planning. To others, such as Rogers, the problem was not that modernism had been too radical, but that it had not been radical enough. That, in the words of Cedric Price describing Harvey Court built in Cambridge in the 1960s by Leslie Martin, 'it was just the Middle Ages with 13 amp power plugs'.

Part of the answer seemed to be to look again at the Modern Movement's most radical phase, to discover if the problem was simply a wrong turning rather than a wrong direction. Rogers was educated against a background in which the revisionist history of modernism was just beginning to be written. Tutors at the Architectural Association such as Alan Colquhoun and James Stirling, through his connections with the academic Colin Rowe, were beginning to look beyond the conventional litany of the Modern Movement masters that was limited to Gropius, Mies van der Rohe, machine-age Le Corbusier, Frank Lloyd Wright and Alvar Aalto. Instead they began to examine the subtler nuances of the Italian rationalists, Adolf Loos, the Futurists and Expressionists and others who had been excluded from the history books because they were not limited by the architecture of the smooth-skinned white cube of the International Style, as defined by Philip Johnson and Henry Russell Hitchock's pre-war New York Museum of Modern Art exhibition.

Rogers was particularly impressed by an early visit he paid in 1958 to the Maison de Verre, Pierre Chareau's *tour de force* of inventive design, inserted into a nineteenth-century Parisian courtyard on the Left Bank. It was a building which in every detail and finish, from the frank expression of its steel I beam structure to the glass brick walls that diffuse controlled light through its interior, reflected a lyrical celebration of the imagery of the machine age. Its studded rubber floor, perforated steel partition walls and free-standing tubular metal channels that carry all the electrical and telephone wires throughout the building, as well as the power sockets and light switches and the immaculately crafted furnishings, were inspired by an optimistic sense of possibilities in industrial culture. This was not simply the mindless mannerism of high-tech. Its spacious and light-filled interior was in distinct contrast to the chilly and uncomfortable insides of Bauhaus buildings, and even today feels as though it would be an exhilarating place in which to live.

The Maison de Verre had been designed by Chareau in the 1930s, yet by the time Rogers paid a visit thirty years later, it remained almost unknown in London. Indeed

Britain was still catching up with the idea that such a thing as 'modern' architecture – by this stage a movement that was in the hands of a third generation of architects – actually existed. The house provided a continuing source of inspiration for Rogers' own buildings and on visiting it as a student he had written: 'This is possibly the least known and the greatest of twentieth-century houses (. . .) it is a building far ahead of its time, and only now is one beginning to realise its influence. Le Corbusier often went to the house while it was being built and it is very close to his concept of a house being "a machine to live in". The work of Stirling, Eames and Prouvé shows the influence of this building. Its means of expression are pertinent to twentieth-century means of expression'.

Rogers belonged to a generation and a mind-set infected by the radicalism of the 1960s – with its refusal to accept received wisdom, or conventional symbols of authority – who saw that something was wrong with much contemporary architecture. But his response to the manifest shortcomings of what was going up all around him was not to reject the idea of modern culture, which in his view took in Freud and Cubism as well as Le Corbusier, but to find alternatives to the reductionism of the commercialised version of modernism in a re-examination of the nature of technology, in the needs of people, and in the idea of accessibility and openness.

Rogers' post-graduate experience in America clearly contributed to his view. At Yale, Rogers met Norman Foster for the first time. Foster had done his architecture degree at Manchester and came from a very different background. But in America he was able, like many Englishmen of his age and experience, to reinvent himself and find an alternative to the aridity of British horizons in the optimism and openness of American life. In those long ago pre-Vietnam War days, Foster discovered Paul Rudolph, Craig Ellwood and Charles Eames who were to inform the two key Team 4 projects: the

America left a lasting impression on architects of Rogers' generation: from the boundless technological self-confidence of Buckminster Fuller that reached its apotheosis in the geodesic dome at the Montreal Expo, *top*, to the poetic modernism of Louis Kahn and his laboratories at Pennsylvania University, *above*.

Piano and Rogers' 1973 factory for the fragrance company, UOP, at Tadworth in Surrey, *right*, draws on the imagery of the machine. With its radius cornered windows and its sleek glass-reinforced cement cladding, it could almost be a piece of industrial design, such as a refrigerator or a television, enlarged to the scale of a building.

house in Cornwall and the Reliance Controls factory. Rogers on the other hand was deeply impressed by the work of Louis Kahn. The monumentalised services distribution system of the Richards laboratories in Philadelphia of 1961, which gave legibility and character to the basic box of academic buildings by taking the service ducts outside the structure, has turned out to be a continuing motif in Rogers' subsequent work. Even when Kahn was first developing the idea of expressing service elements as huge brick boxes, Colin St John Wilson was raising an objection that would subsequently be levelled at Rogers' recurring use of exposed services as scale-making devices. 'Will "servant spaces" be the next form of decoration?', he asked in a critical piece on the Richards building in the pages of *Perspecta* magazine in 1961. Le Corbusier clearly would not have wanted that. Reyner Banham quoted him in *The Architecture of the Well-Tempered Environment*: 'I do not like ducts, I do not like pipes. I hate them really thoroughly, but because I hate them so thoroughly, I feel they have to be given their place. If I just hated them and took no care, I think that they would invade the building, and completely destroy it.' So by that definition at least, Rogers' architecture has to be seen as something rather different from what was the modern mainstream.

Neither Rogers nor Foster were architectural intellectuals. Both were intuitive designers, driven primarily by the exhilaration of building and creating space and form, rather than by any sense of overwhelming commitment to theory. They went along with the fashionable ideas of their times, and made some discoveries of their own. Both were seduced, at least for a time, by Buckminster Fuller with his utopian espousal of structure and technology. Rogers, predisposed to rebelliousness and with a strong independence of mind, did not take kindly to the idea of architecture as an imposed, hierarchical system. He valued openness and accessibility above almost everything else. The lack of hierarchy implied by the free plan and the sense of honesty that came from a refusal to apply a cosmetic façade but to express the essential nature of the building beneath felt instinctively right to Rogers. The idea of basing a building's plan on the conventional notions of architectural composition was anathema. Originality and innovation were important in themselves. Buildings that were dominated by routine hierarchical circulation patterns, by corridors and cell-like rooms were, to Rogers, much less interesting than buildings which had a chance to develop a theatrical sense of space, characterised by big dramatic single volumes and the flamboyant use of colour. There was also a boyish enthusiasm in his work for achieving technically difficult feats with as much nonchalance as possible. For Rogers it seemed that architecture should be like a progressive education, a self-directed process of discovery, rather than a disciplined, pre-ordained sequence of formal lessons.

Rogers was always enthusiastic about the liberating potential of technology. The craft skills of the building industry seemed to him to represent no more than

drudgery and antediluvian incompetence. Why not sweep it away with prefabrication and factory-style automation? This was hardly the first time that such a proposition had been formulated. The idea of stamping houses out on production lines had been one of the on-going dreams of the modernists since the early years of the century. The German wing of the Modern Movement had achieved something like its image – reducing modernism to pristine white boxes that looked as if they might be the product of a rational machine-age process, even if they were in fact nothing of the kind and relied on laborious handcraft skills. At the other end of the spectrum were the Italian Futurists, who were more interested in the poetic possibilities of the romance of the machine, but seldom troubled to ground their speculations in reality.

This interest in the poetic possibilities of the modern world had inspired Britain's most feverish architectural avant-garde group, Archigram. But unlike the Italians, the English were more excited by rockets and computers than steam engines and early bi-planes. Based at the Architectural Association in the years just after Rogers had left, Archigram numbered Peter Cook, Warren Chalk, Ron Herron, Dennis Crompton, Michael Webb and David Greene among its members. Warren Chalk summed up their position as follows: 'We are in pursuit of an idea, a new vernacular, something to stand alongside the space capsules, computers and throwaway packages of an atomic, electronic age. We are not trying to make houses like cars, or cities like oil refineries. This analogous imagery will eventually be digested into a creative system. It has become necessary to extend ourselves into such disciplines in order to discover our appropriate language for the present day situation.

Ron Herron designed a 'walking city' in 1964, a project based on a memorable series of drawings that took the megastructure, the fashionable motif of the time, and

Completed in 1970, the house that Rogers designed for his parents at Wimbledon Common, *left and below*, combines an elegant, minimal steel structure with maximum glazing, to provide a home with an interior that has a scale and space sympathetic to the way of life of its owners.

rendered it at the scale of a city, turning it in the process into a vast wheeled object. Peter Cook produced his blueprint for the Plug-In City – a series of drawings that showed a complex made up not exactly of skyscrapers but of frameworks into which standardised components accommodating housing or offices could be slotted. Function here was to be given shape not by form, but by mechanical and electronic services. It was an image that was strikingly close to the services wall of the Pompidou on its street frontage. Archigram, unlike the Futurists, always maintained a sense of irony and wit. While the messianic Marinetti's celebration of speed and technology had blurred uncomfortably easily into the authoritarian war worship of the Fascists. Archigram members were fascinated by pop culture and the aesthetics of American consumerism rather than utopia.

Cedric Price worked along parallel lines to Archigram on some of his speculative projects – the Fun Palace and the Potteries think-belt project in particular. The latter was an attempt to abolish not just monumental buildings but any sense of place, by distributing a university along a road and railway network. Price had more of the rhetoric of social commitment; Archigram were studiously value-free pranksters. In fact, none of them constructed anything that came close to achieving the radicalism of their drawings. In many ways the first Archigram building actually realised can be considered to be the Pompidou Centre. Despite winning a competition to design an entertainments centre in Monte Carlo, Archigram never really built anything, though some of its members played a large part in the design of London's South Bank cultural centre. But this did not diminish Archigram's reputation, and the group became internationally famous well before Rogers. This was still a period during which it was possible to enjoy a substantial critical reputation as an architect without building at all. And Archigram's images were especially popular in Japan and Italy, where they

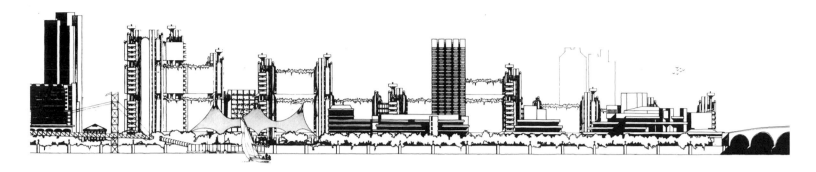

The Coin Street redevelopment on London's South Bank became a *cause célèbre* in planning, the focus of a ritualised conflict between those who saw themselves as safeguarding the interests of the community, and the developers. In the middle was the Rogers office, which spent five years patiently refining plans for a mix of offices, shops and housing, *above*, that would have brought a metropolitan scale to the long-neglected riverfront. In the event the project, with its gallerias and towers that appeared in the massing of the Lloyds' building was abandoned. The site was turned over to low-rise social housing.

inspired equally visionary groups including Archizoom and Superstudio. Drawings alone could be enough to make some architects famous, and indeed there was a perverse tendency for those who maintained their purity by confining themselves to drawing and teaching to look with a certain disdain at those who were prepared to move out of the realms of theory and make the compromises that building demanded.

Price and Archigram were even more hard-nosed and uncompromising about what constituted architecture than the Smithsons, and completely opposed to the idea of conventional buildings. Price was prepared to speculate on the pointlessness of spending huge sums on conserving cathedrals and, presciently, wrote of the impossibility of conventional design and construction methods being able to deliver buildings that were anything but redundant by the time they were actually finished. This point was given flesh by Rogers in his attempts to reflect the varying life expectancy of building components in physical form, and has been demonstrated over and over again by airports planned for turbo props and then swamped by jets as soon as they open; by office buildings overtaken by the demands of information technology before they are even occupied; and even by the new British Library, thirty years in the building and emerging finally as a dinosaur of the book age in an era in which information is digitised, not transmitted on paper. It was this kind of thinking that led to such transitory 1970s phenomena as the obsession with inflatable structures, which for a while became the badge of courage of the architectural student trying to make a mark. These were credited with mystical powers of transformation as was the building that came in a box and could be erected instantly, in which form took care of itself, and the builder was irrelevant.

The early 1960s had been shaped by an uncomplicated enthusiasm for technologically inspired architecture. In Japan there were Arata Isozaki's metabolist drawings of 1964, and the capsule structures of Kisho Kurokawa. These certainly seemed to anticipate the motifs of the Lloyd's building in particular, in the way that they gave physical expression to the techniques of prefabrication. Yona Friedman designed a space-frame megastructure that went spilling out all over Paris in 1963. Buckminster Fuller's huge geodesic dome, the Climatron, was designed in 1962 to enclose Manhattan. Ezra Ehrenkrantz and Robertson Ward produced the prototype Southern Californian Schools District structure in Palo Alto in the same year. Against this background, Rogers' thinking was hardly out of the mainstream. but what distinguished him from his peers was getting to build the Pompidou, and having the stamina and the help to turn it into a beautiful object that was actually more impressive than the design drawings.

Rogers finally graduated in 1961, and in the ten years that passed before he won the Pompidou competition with Renzo Piano, he lists just fourteen projects in his portfolio.

One of them, a conservatory-cum-retreat at Pill Wood in Cornwall is no more than a glass shelter, a kind of aircraft cockpit sunk into a headland at Feock and built as work got under way on the main Brumwell house at Creek Vean. Only seven of the fourteen were actually completed. Apart from Reliance Controls there was another small factory, the 1969 Universal Oil Products (UOP) building in Ashford, Kent, which was one of the first glass-reinforced cement buildings in Britain. This material, which was used to make precast cladding panels, briefly caught Rogers' imagination as a material of the future, but its technical shortcomings prevented its wide application.

With the exception of the two factories and the extension for Design Research Unit, the other projects built before the Pompidou were domestic. The Brumwell house was followed by another, this time for his own parents in Wimbledon. Designed with Su Rogers, it is a handsome, vivid yellow, painted steel structure, with a gate house forming a protective courtyard in front and a lushly landscaped garden beyond. In California or Australia, where society is less prejudiced against the idea of building new houses, it would have fitted easily into the background. In Britain this pair of dwellings was exceptional, and confidently demonstrated how much the single-storey, open-plan way of life had to offer. They provided a handsome setting for everyday life, where Eames chairs and pre-war furniture designed by Ernesto Rogers could happily co-exist.

During the many quiet periods in these early years, when paid commissions dried up completely, Rogers carried out a series of speculative technical explorations. The best known of these were the two Zip-Up houses, that looked into prefabrication, dry assembly methods and autonomous structures, in which the use of high-performance insulation materials reduce the need for external energy to a miserly minimum. Rogers was certain that, for him, architectural development was not to be measured in shifts of emphasis in stylistic and formal mannerisms, but was essentially a matter of social

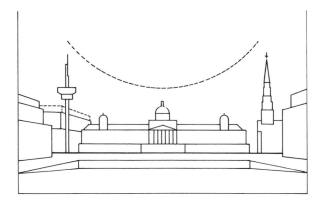

It is likely that it was the Rogers design for the National Gallery extension competition that provoked the intervention of the Prince of Wales in the architectural world with his 'Carbuncle' speech, ushering in the fruitless confrontation of competing styles that dominated the next few years. Rogers' design was a deliberate attempt to treat Trafalgar Square as a three-dimensional composition, introducing a turret to balance the spire of St Martin-in-the-Fields, *top and left*, and providing a pedestrian link into the centre of the square.

and technical invention. It was not that he was uninterested in history, but as far as he was concerned: 'It is those periods when change quickens and turning points are reached, when innovation is more important than consolidation and the perfecting of style, that interest me most. I prefer Brunelleschi to Michelangelo, Early English Gothic to its decorated successor, Borromini to the historicism that followed.'

The carnival spirit of the streets when, for a few weeks in May 1968, it seemed that some kind of epochal shift in attitudes and possibilities was really taking place, deeply affected Rogers. The Pompidou was really an attempt to institutionalise the quasi-insurrectionary take-over of the Sorbonne and the Comédie Française by the students in 1968, when rock concerts, political debates, teach-ins, be-ins and street theatre spontaneously erupted along the Left Bank twenty-four hours a day. But that hope quickly died and Rogers, like many liberals of the period, found himself in danger of becoming part of the problem rather than part of the solution, at least in the eyes of the more doctrinaire radicals.

Throughout a large part of his career, Rogers has seen himself as an outsider. When he was starting out in practice, the first ten years of his career were erratic. There was barely enough work to keep the studio going for some periods, and he had to supplement his income by teaching. By the time the Pompidou was completed, the cultural climate had changed and the very anti-elitism that Rogers championed was a force that was being turned against the architectural profession as a whole. Architects – for generations unchallenged figures of authority – found themselves under attack. Technical shortcomings in architecture and cynical and manipulative urban development were strongly opposed by Rogers. But there were those who saw the Pompidou as representing not the total accessibility that Rogers espoused but technology running riot and viewed its design as inhuman and mechanistic, and counter to the urban grain of the area and its architectural context.

The building was indeed the subject of furious controversy. It had both its partisans and its implacable opponents. Prefabrication, high-rises and modernism in general were all under attack during this period. Rogers found himself on the defensive, forced to speak out against post-modernism and in favour of a continued belief in the potential of technology and modernism. 'If post-modernism originally represented a protest against the monotony and alienating character of much modern, in particular International Style, architecture, it has rapidly become the superficial aesthetic of shoddy commercial design. Its sympathy for historicism has degenerated all too often into a shallow decoration, a self-indulgent playing with symbols, which has no integral relation with the functions of the building, but succeeds in disguising its fundamental poverty. If post-modernist publications tend to dwell on elevations it is because plan and section, the stuff of the best modern architecture, have been entirely given over to

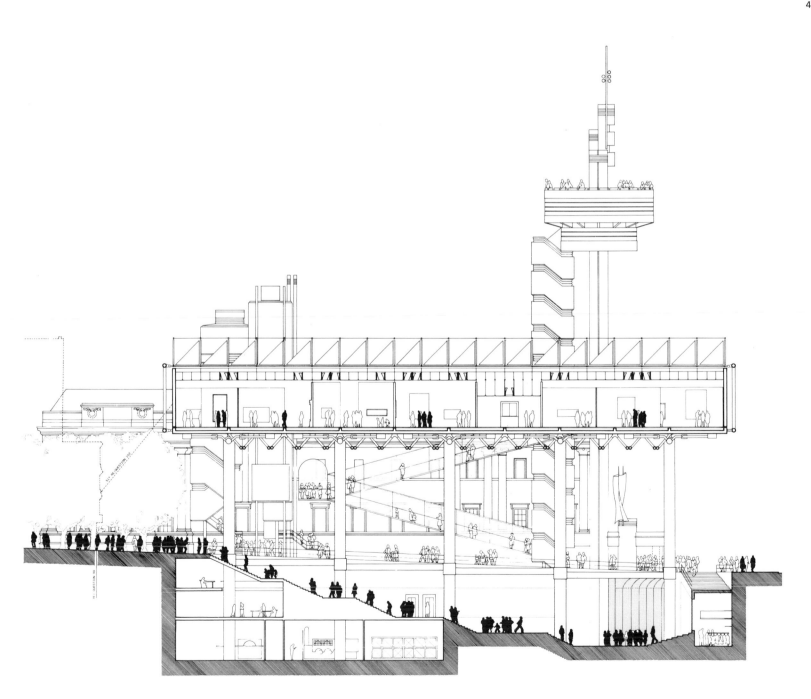

The partnership's submission for the competition to redevelop Paternoster Square around St Paul's, *opposite*, was to prove as controversial as its National Gallery design, *above*. Though the judges were impressed by the idea of scooping open the space above the adjoining underground station to provide travellers with a spectacular view of the cathedral, the Prince made it quite clear that it would get no support from him.

the maximisation of rentable space', he wrote in his book *Architecture: A Modern View*, published by Thames & Hudson in 1990.

It is hardly surprising that Rogers began to feel more than a little embattled. His first major urban scheme in which planning counted as much as architecture was the Coin Street development on the south bank of the Thames. It was designed at the end of the 1970s, but became the focus for one of the bitterest planning battles of the period, with Rogers cast as the developer's apologist by the opposition, which was funded by the Greater London Council. In fact this was one of the first big schemes of Stuart Lipton, the developer who was later to recast the shape of commercial office complexes in London with the Broadgate project. The radicals demanded small-scale housing, workshops and factories – the elements they considered essential to keep life in the centre of London. Rogers, on the other hand, responded to the urbanity of the site with a project that mixed offices, retail space and housing, stretching in a long sweeping crescent to culminate in a new bridge across the Thames. Above all, it was of a scale and size that responded to what Rogers called the metropolitan character of the riverside site. In the end, after years of legal wrangling, demonstrations and invective, the developers backed out, and the site was handed over to a state-funded social housing group.

Rogers was also in the thick of the other great architectural row of the 1980s: the long drawn-out fiasco of the National Gallery extension. It was this experience that first brought him into conflict with the Prince of Wales, whose relentlessly publicised incursion into the architectural arena in 1984 was triggered by the competition for the design of a new wing for the gallery in Trafalgar Square.

'Prince Charles and his followers have been praised for focusing attention on the wretched nature of many British townscapes and landscapes. But by limiting their attack to a question of superficial style, and by blaming architects alone, these critics have avoided finding any fault with the political and financial reality, the fact that architectural patronage and urban planning are in the hands of commercial and political bodies for whom quality appears to be a very low priority,' said Rogers giving the Walter Neurath Memorial Lecture in 1989.

Rogers' submission for the competition held in 1982 was extraordinary, setting its face against the increasingly cautious and contextual climate of the times. This was a period before full-blooded neo-classicism had made its appearance. Quinlan Terry had yet to complete his bizarre development at Richmond-on-Thames with its literal recreation of period façades concealing open-plan speculative office interiors, but architecture was nonetheless in the grip of a kind of crisis of confidence. This was the height of the vernacular revival, the era of let-us-all-be-quiet-as-little-mice architecture. It was axiomatic that brick and slate and pitched roofs were friendly, and steel and

49

concrete were not. Even in this climate Rogers stuck to his guns, determined to design another building that would have the same kind of impact as the Pompidou. Ignoring the fact that the assessors for the competition included Hugh Casson, and that the gallery staff themselves were interested in a building with the character of a basilica to house a fine collection of Renaissance art, Rogers pulled out all the stops and submitted an entry which made even sympathetic architects' jaws drop. The most prominent element was the tower, a kind of high-tech spire more than 150 feet high that was a deliberate riposte to the spire of St Martin's-in-the-Field across Trafalgar Square, and to Nelson's Column in its centre. The tower was designed to incorporate one of the steel-clad semi-detached staircases which are such a prominent feature of Lloyd's, but there are also hints of the enthusiasms of members of the Rogers office for a kind of 1930s streamlining that descends directly from Erich Mendelsohn's work. This tendency re-emerged in the design for Whittington Avenue which runs next to the Lloyd's building in the City of London.

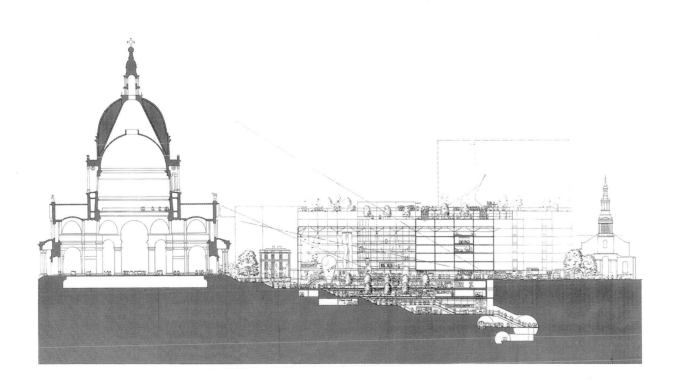

The brief for the National Gallery extension was hatched by Michael Heseltine in his days as Minister for the Environment. It specified that the building must contain enough commercial office space to fund the additional galleries that the museum needed. To this end, Rogers proposed two distinct spatial systems for the building, hoisting the galleries up into the air in a stone-faced, steel-framed, top-lit box, while the offices would have been in a serpentine curtain-walled structure beneath. But perhaps most radical of all was Rogers' proposal to tinker with the urban grain of London in a way that would help to make the area the kind of social magnet that the Pompidou has become. The tower would have had restaurants and cafés on top of it, offering some of the most spectacular views of London's most famous landmarks. Rogers also identified the site as a key part of a new pedestrian route that could link two of London's great undervalued public spaces: Trafalgar Square and Leicester Square. The first functioned as little more than a traffic roundabout, used for occasional political demonstrations and New Year celebrations; the second was equally unattractive and, despite being pedestrianised, just as cut-off from the rest of London. While the two sites feel psychologically worlds apart, they are only yards away from each other. Rogers proposed a new north-south route linking the two, taking pedestrians down a ramped outdoor space into a new mall passing underneath the roadway on the north side of Trafalgar Square and out through a new opening into the square itself, thereby ending its traffic-inflicted isolation. A stunning coup, it would have produced a genuinely memorable design, instead of the mannered and unsatisfactory compromise designed by Robert Venturi and Denise Scott Brown.

This site was the subject of the great 'Carbuncle' speech. Prince Charles seized the architectural initiative at Hampton Court in 1984, and far from delivering the anodyne platitudes expected of him, chose to make a highly controversial and opinionated assault, mocking the winning design for the site by Ahrends Burton and Koralek as a carbuncle on the face of an old friend. ABK might well have produced the chosen scheme, but it was widely believed that the prince had been referring to that of Rogers. The speech changed the face of British architecture for a decade, and left Rogers initially winded, then mute, and finally increasingly outspoken in his condemnation of the prince's ever more shrill interventions. It was years before he finally shook off the cloud of being seen as occupying top position on the prince's hit list.

There was to be another equally damaging intervention by the prince directly against Rogers in the Paternoster Square competition in 1987, which led to the dropping of first Rogers, and later Arup Associates, from the winning ticket. This was a major project for a site whose future still hadn't been determined five years later. Rather than allow the office space, and the jobs that went with them, to slip away to Docklands, the City's planners declared open season on buildings from the 1960s. Stuart Lipton, the developer, organised a limited competition for rebuilding Paternoster, with a list of participants that included Rogers, Foster and Stirling, as well as Arata Isozaki from Japan. Perhaps in a bid to head off criticism from the prince, who by this time had become an unofficial arbiter of public taste and was showing every sign of enjoying his new found power, Lipton showed him the finalists' designs before the judges had made their decision public. Predictably the intervention of the prince saw the victory, if that is what it can really be called, go to Arup Associates' comparatively classical design. (Arups' idea was later displaced, however, in favour of a still more literal recreation of London's past proposed by a new set of developers.) But there was one element of Rogers' entry that the assessors could not ignore, a kind of magnification of the proposal to burrow into Trafalgar Square. Here Rogers proposed opening up a great glass cavern on top of the underground station so that you would gradually rise up on escalators and find yourself coming face to face with the sublime view of the cathedral.

For a while it seemed that the Rogers office had become too controversial to get commissions from any clients not prepared to stand their ground and fight furiously for their right to choose the architect's ideas. It became necessary, and a great deal easier, for the Richard Rogers Partnership to look for work in France, Japan and Germany. There was even a flurry of activity by opponents of Rogers to withdraw planning permission for Lloyd's half-way through its construction, on the grounds that the project as actually being built deviated from the original design that had been approved. Uncowed, Rogers quietly fought back, helping to create a constituency for a more enlightened approach to architecture. As time has passed, the climate has changed again, the perception of Rogers has shifted with it, and his workload has once again expanded within Britain.

3 | From Pompidou to Lloyd's

The Pompidou Centre was by far the most talked about piece of new architecture of the 1970s. At a time when the abstraction of contemporary architecture had made it one of the most difficult of the arts for the wider public to appreciate, the Pompidou entered the popular imagination in a way that few could have predicted. Architecture had become arcane, something that, despite its ubiquity, was like a private language. Yet the Pompidou broke through all this, and received a positive response from both the public and the professionals. Representing modernism's only true success of the decade, it attracted not just architectural initiates from all over the world, but also crowds on a scale that eclipsed the Louvre and the Eiffel tower combined, and quickly earned a place in every guide book to Paris as an unmissable attraction. And no wonder, since it includes the finest view over the centre of the city from its glass-encased escalators, free of charge. It has become one of the key images of the city in front of which tourists pose for photographs as proof of their travels. It has inspired the designs of album covers and table lamps, and formed the backdrop for advertisements promoting Renault and Mercedes. It has been reproduced in the form of cardboard cut-out kits and used as the set for a Bond film. It is in short an icon, a bridge between high and popular culture.

The Pompidou's impact remains undiminished today, even as it begins to mature into middle age. The constant tread of up to 70,000 visitors' feet each day may have made threadbare and shopsoiled large slices of its most heavily trafficked areas. Gae Aulenti may have been called in to remodel the floors on which France's principal collection of contemporary art is housed to create a setting closer to a conventional gallery than the wide open spaces that Piano and Rogers provided, and a thorough refurbishment programme has been mooted. But the sheer forcefulness and verve of the structure is as strong as ever. As a public space, the open square in front of the building, envisaged

While its flamboyant structure, left, attracted most of the attention when the Pompidou Centre opened in 1977, that was only one aspect of the building. Just as important was its ability to attract crowds to the large open square in front of it that was an integral part of the design.

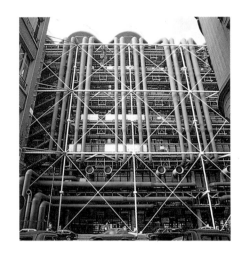

The best free view of Paris still attracts countless thousands of sightseers up the Pompidou's escalators, *opposite*, many of whom never set foot inside its museums. The street front of the Pompidou with its notorious colour-coded exposed plumbing, *above, and opposite page, top,* made explicit the realities of modern building.

by the architects as being of as much importance as the building itself, remains unmatched in its magnetic attraction for people of all kinds.

The architectural competition for the Pompidou was launched in 1970, the result of an initiative by the French president after whom it is named. Piano and Rogers were selected from 681 entries in July 1971 by a jury that included Philip Johnson and Jean Prouvé, and the former directors of the British Museum in London and the Stedelijk in Amsterdam. The brief was for a cultural centre for Paris that would include a library, design centre and cinema, as well as gallery space for fine art and studios for music. Given that Rogers had had to be persuaded by his partner to enter the competition in the first place because he saw little prospect of designing anything but a monument to the highly centralised French state, it's hardly surprising that the written report accompanying their submission deliberately set out to subvert the brief. Piano and Rogers refer not to a 'cultural centre', but a 'live centre for information and entertainment', a formula with a very different emphasis, one which would be 'a combination of the British Museum and Times Square'. They go on to describe, 'a flexible container, and a dynamic communications machine made from prefabricated parts to attract as wide a public as possible by cutting across traditional institutional limits; a people's centre, a university of the street.'

The rhetoric shows how much of an impact the events of May 1968 had on Piano and Rogers. When the very word museum became anathema as it did in the 1960s, no one dreamed of suggesting that a museum should look like a museum. By the time the Pompidou opened in 1977, the pendulum was beginning to swing in the other direction: the idea of archetype and precedent was once more part of the architectural agenda. Some critics, notably Rogers' one-time tutor Alan Colquhoun accused the Pompidou of abdicating its civic role by refusing to present a formal, public façade. Museum design for a while became a series of variations on the theme originally defined in the nineteenth century by Schinkel, a move that culminated in James Stirling's Staatsgalerie in Stuttgart. Now the picture is changing again: the idea of creating a specifically modern expression for a museum is seen once more as an issue. The Pompidou has survived both swings with its reputation intact. It has a validity that transcends any particular nuance of architectural fashion.

The original drawings showed a façade covered with electronic signage systems, giant video screens and interactive art – ideas that recall some of the pioneering pieces of modernism from the 1930s, such as Rietveld's glass and neon façade for the Vreeburg Cinema in Utrecht. The architecturally scaled advertisements of Tokyo in the 1980s have brought this to life in the electronic age, but the idea proved too much for the Parisian authorities to accept, and they vetoed Piano and Rogers' proposals for their inclusion. As built, the centre is not quite the open-ended structure that Piano

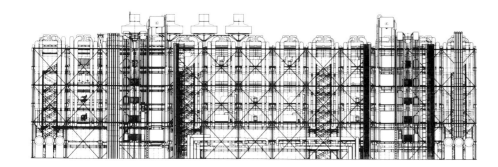

and Rogers proposed. Cost savings and the rigid interpretation of the implications of the provisions of the fire regulations meant the omission of most of the open voids that the original design contained. On the other hand, the climbing-frame steel façade with its escalator tube slashing diagonally up and across is there, so too is the stunning services wall on the rue Renard. Inside, the column-free structure allows for the display of everything from Mirage jet fighters to Matisse paintings.

During the run-up to the start of the building programme, the project went through a number of redesigns. In essence the original scheme was initially discarded when the fire services objected to the height of the building. A truncated version was designed, which would have lacked the power and impact of the final structure, and a third option was finally evolved, going back to many of the original ideas in the competition design. As built, the Pompidou has a large bookshop, a roof-top café and restaurant, a design store and a continuous cinema programme. And of course, it has some of the most powerful works of twentieth-century art in the world. In many ways, it is the model for the way that the museum has evolved in the second half of the twentieth century; no longer is it an entirely didactic institution, or a trophy house maintained in the interests of national prestige, but a temple of consumerism. Piano and Rogers established a team to research ways of giving the centre a wider mix of activities. As a result, the new museum has become an urban landmark, a replacement for the missing agora, devoted to spectacle and providing people with a place to meet, talk, look, eat, drink and shop.

Piano and Rogers' design brought home just how far the museum could be pushed towards becoming a public space. 'In our eyes, the square was as important as the building. In a city as dense as Paris, we thought it was important not to occupy the whole of the available site, rather we tried to create a sort of clearing in which you

From the start it was always envisaged that the flexibility of the Pompidou's interior would encourage changes in its use as time went by. Gae Aulenti was called in to remodel some of the original gallery spaces in 1986, *opposite*, to provide a sense of solidity, and a scale that was closer to the setting in which the pictures on show would once have been seen. The heavy traffic of visitors has taken its toll, but planned maintenance programmes are being implemented to restore the original freshness of the colours and materials.

could see activity and life that complemented what was going on inside the centre. And we planned to link the space with an underpass to Les Halles, which at that time we never believed would be demolished.'

For Rogers, it is precisely the fire-eaters and the buskers and the stallholders in the outside piazza who bring the Pompidou to life. 'The movement and the fun have an essential role, just as they do in the open spaces of Italy. If you take away the activity in the piazzas of Florence and Siena, you have nothing left. The square in front of the Pompidou works in exactly the same way.'

The Pompidou was conceived by two architects intoxicated with the rhetoric of impermanence and flexibility. Explicit in the design was the idea that the museum was a focus for people and spectacle, as much as a place for instruction or enlightenment. It was seen from the outset as a magnet for the social life of a city, designed as a crowd-pleaser, attracting countless thousands of visitors who would have no intention of looking at the art contained within its sparse walls. But the Pompidou is not just an aesthetically extraordinary building; it is also a considerable technical achievement. One of the first battles that Piano and Rogers fought, and won, shortly after their victory in the competition, was to gain full responsibility for the detailed design of the entire structure rather than being limited to conceptual design only, as is common in France. This allowed them to work with the engineers at Ove Arup to create a structure based on some of the largest steel castings ever attempted. Beautiful as objects in in their own right, it is these castings that allow a 48-metre column-free span.

The fire authorities had a major impact on both the form of the building (causing the overall height to be lowered), and the materials used. Piano and Rogers have filled the hollow steel columns with water to serve as a fire protection system. (They tried to use the idea for the Lloyd's building too, but didn't persuade the authorities to accept it, although it has been used in smaller scale buildings designed by other architects.) The rest of the Pompidou's elegant steel work is carefully wrapped in fireproof quilted blankets, which in turn are hidden inside a steel sleeve. What you see when you look at the building, both inside and out, may look like an exposed steel structure, but in fact is not. However, this is being re-examined as part of a continuing maintenance and refurbishment programme of the building and at the time of writing it seemed likely that the applied fire protection would eventually be removed.

More seriously compromising to the original concept was the partial compartmentalisation of the interior insisted on by the fire regulations. The initial idea was for a huge open interior that could be adapted to any new use. As built, there are partitions which compromise, although they do not entirely rule out, that flexibility. Nonetheless, even if the Pompidou does not exactly represent Piano and Rogers' initial vision, that cannot detract from the fact that it is an immense achievement. The

64

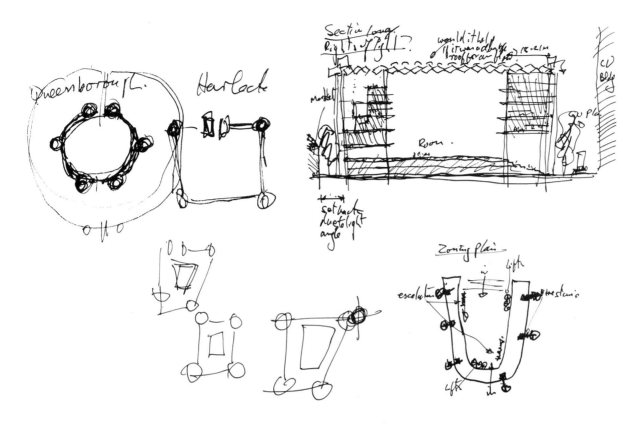

The partnership won the commission for the Lloyd's building on the strength of its strategy for dealing with the forecast growth of the institution, rather than with a detailed design. Early sketches by Rogers, *left*, explored the possibility of a building in which services, stairs and lifts were all pulled out of the main shell. This would free up the interior and offer the possibility of an exterior given much more scale and incident than is conventionally possible with a bland and anonymous office block. The form, as eventually realised, *below*, put Rogers at least in mind of the castles of medieval England, though the stair turrets, *opposite*, suggest a more technological image.

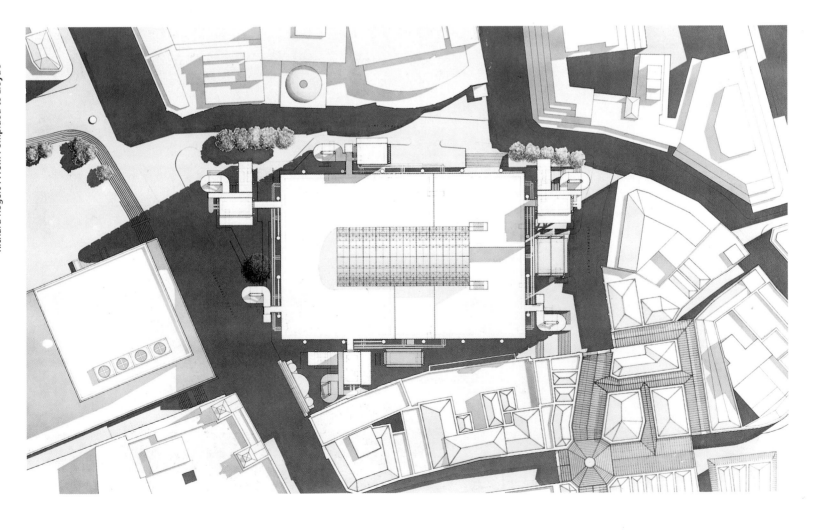

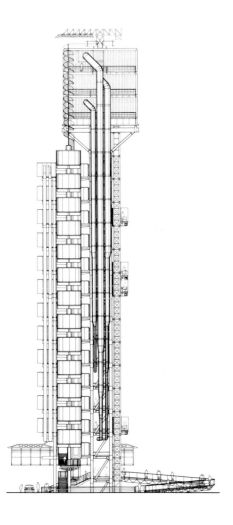

structure is there, put together with the delicacy of jewellery on an industrial scale; the expressed services envisaged in the design have been realised intact; and, most important, the street life is there.

It has to be said, though, that the area is not quite the joyous university of the streets that Rogers imagined, but is now marked by the constant shuffle of tourists moving back and forth between the shopping centre of Les Halles and the Pompidou, from fast food restaurant to sex shop to postcard stand. Meanwhile the area's residents have complained endlessly about the constant noise, not from the Latin American flute players and the colourful fire eaters, but from street people miming to ghetto blasters and psychotic heavy metal guitarists plugged into amplifiers. There are certainly people in the streets: Rogers has succeeded only too well in bringing them here. But there are times when the whole area feels more like a triumph of passive consumerism, rather than a tribute to dynamic public participation; an area crowded with aimless tourists, rather than the focus for a genuine metropolitan culture.

Interestingly, the design as realised is far more elegant and composed than the original rather crude model and the simple drawings suggested. It must have taken a considerable leap of faith on the part of the judges to see the potential of what Piano and Rogers promised in the unseductive images that they presented. Yet such confidence paid off. For once modernism, or at least the romantic view of it represented by the Pompidou, proved genuinely popular, and it can be seen as triggering off an important shift in French architecture in particular, which at the start of the 1970s was in the doldrums, in the wake of the death of Le Corbusier. The radicalism of the Pompidou provoked not just imitators, but a whole school of architects interested in pushing design in a technological, dynamic direction, from Jean Nouvel to Dominique Perrault. Twenty years later, by the beginning of the 1990s,

Despite initial scepticism, and the tarnishing of Lloyd's own reputation, the building has become an authentic landmark of the new London, *opposite*. With its extraordinary silhouette it has been cast by some as the personification of technologically driven change. But in fact, it is still the product of a traditional brief: a city centre headquarters for an owner-occupier. The cut may be eccentric, but it is still a Savile Row suit.

France had emerged as a country in which some of the most tirelessly energetic experiments in architectural form anywhere in the world could be found. The Pompidou was the godfather of the *Grand Projets* of President Mitterrand, and the catalyst of its many provincial emulators, from Nouvel's Opera House in Lyons to Norman Foster's Maison Carrée in Nîmes, both completed in 1993. And it gave birth to a whole stream of architecture that self-consciously set out to explore the limits of technology and form in shaping new buildings.

What the Pompidou did not do, however, was to provide Richard Rogers with any more work after it was completed. Even in France, where its success might have been expected to bring him a choice of further projects, it took several years before Rogers secured any new commissions besides the Fleetguard factory in Brittany in 1980. Perhaps it was something to do with Renzo Piano's decision to set up a permanent base in Paris, when Rogers went back to London in 1975, that meant it was Piano who picked up the residual work after the Pompidou was completed, and went on to build the Schlumberger building in Paris.

A decade on, France did become important for Rogers, with commissions from the new Marseilles Airport completed in 1992 and the courthouse in Bordeaux in 1993. But the work didn't just take a while to materialise, it did not provide any real indications for the future direction of Rogers' approach to design. When he finished work on the Pompidou and returned to London, there were a few jobs to finish off: the PA Technology Centre outside Cambridge, and a little known new town housing project. But by the end of the 1970s things were serious enough for Rogers to be on the point of shutting up shop altogether, and packing his bags for a professorship he had been offered in America.

Rescue came at the last moment in the surprising form of a commission to build a new headquarters for Lloyd's of London, not an institution that had previously demonstrated much interest in contemporary architecture. Rogers and his partners, John Young and Marco Goldschmied, had entered a limited architectural competition for the project just as Piano and Rogers were quietly dismantling their partnership. 'We have,' said Rogers at the time, 'been very lucky.' But if the Lloyd's building assured the continued survival of the practice, there have been other issues almost as fundamental for it to face up to. There are those who argue that the philosophy the Pompidou represents is not architecture at all. Rather than exploring issues of spatial complexity, formality and order with the floor plan, the Pompidou in the anti-authoritarian manner typical of its time rejects any such structuring, and instead offers huge open interiors, free of interruptions, to be modified in any way in which the users see fit. The exterior, too, deliberately turns its back on the traditional idea of a museum, eschewing the temple in favour of the aesthetics of engineering structures.

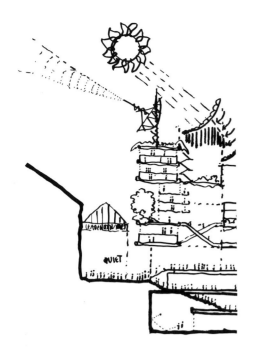

But to Rogers, it is taken as a given that institutions change much more quickly than the buildings that house them. Therefore it is essential for those buildings to be easily changeable in order to accommodate such shifts in use. The aesthetic strategy adopted for the Lloyd's building is rather different. The images that Rogers used when talking about it, by contrast with the radicalism of the Pompidou, were of Street's gothic towers for the Victorian Law Courts in London and the Galleria in Milan, not oil refineries or space shuttles. Meanwhile, the plans for Lloyd's squeaked through the system just ahead of a sudden hardening of attitudes within the City of London. The chances of such a scheme being approved in the early 1980s would have been minimal, as the Rogers office discovered when it attempted to get planning permission for a new commercial development during 1984 in Leadenhall Street.

The balance of power between those people in Britain who want to build things, and those who want to stop them has shifted back and forth with bewildering speed. At the end of the 1970s, Richard Rogers was able to overcome conservationist criticism of his plans to demolish the imperial splendour of Sir Edwin Cooper's 1928 Lloyd's building by personally presenting his designs to the then chairman of Save Britain's Heritage, Marcus Binney, and convincing him to withdraw his objections. Five years later, Binney succeeded in quashing Peter Palumbo's plans to build Mies van der Rohe's posthumous Mansion House Square project. In that short space of time, so entrenched had the presumption become that any building more than thirty years old was worth saving from demolition rather than making way for a new design, no matter how distinguished, that Rogers would have had trouble getting past the City planners, let alone steering the Lloyd's design successfully through a public inquiry.

Shortly after Binney's victory over Mies, the picture was of course quickly reversed by the plans of a consortium of American banks to construct an alternative financial centre for London in Docklands, outside the reach of the restrictions of the planning system. It was a move that concentrated minds in the City. Faced with the prospect of losing important financial institutions, a renewed flexibility once more showed itself. Timing, however, is crucial in such matters, and back in 1978, Rogers was fortunate indeed to get his timing right. The Lloyd's design had all the approvals that it needed, without having to be submitted to a public inquiry, and without any aesthetic compromises.

The story of Lloyd's clearly demonstrates how quickly architecture can become redundant, even in the hands of such tradition-minded institutions. Edwin Cooper's building of 1928 was followed by a replacement built on a site next door, designed by Terence Heysham in 1958, though its anaemic classicism is so archaic that one might be excused for believing it to be half a century older. But in 1978, when Lloyd's was facing up to the troubling prospect of outgrowing its underwriting room for the third

The idea of allowing for future growth of the Room, Lloyd's main work space, by linking floors with escalators rising as far up the atrium as required, came early in the design process, *opposite*, but changes in the technological demands on the structure meant that modifications were made to the cross-section, *below right*, even after construction work had begun.

time in fifty years, it was in the mood for more radical solutions. It had already taken the decisive step of moving a substantial part of its clerical operations to a computer centre in Chatham. To ensure that continuing growth did not force it to make yet another rapid move, it went to the Royal Institute of British Architects, fortunately presided over by Gordon Graham at that time, for advice on choosing a suitable architect. From a shortlist that included Arup Associates, Norman Foster and I.M. Pei, Lloyd's chose Rogers, not because of a specific design proposal, for he had prepared nothing more than concept diagrams, but for the evidence he gave the company of the way in which he would approach the design.

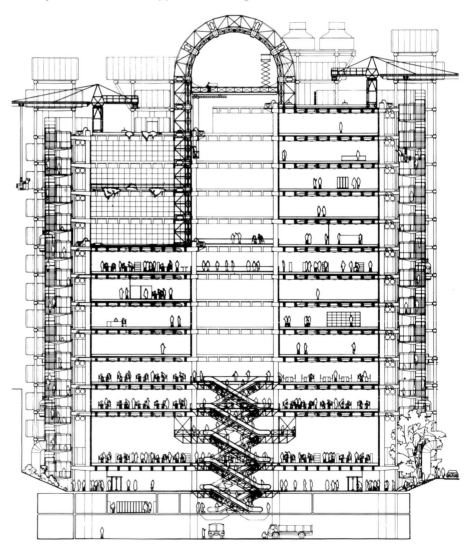

Lloyd's is in essence a market place, run with quintessential British amateurism as a species of gentleman's club, still shaped in its practices by the traditions of the original coffee house after which Lloyd's is named. It is a forum in which underwriters organised into syndicates gather to set up stalls to do business with insurance brokers looking for cover for their clients. Like any market, personal contact is vital, and it is that consideration which has dictated that Lloyd's continues to be centred in one single underwriting room. The continual growth of the business and the rising number of underwriters wishing to work there in the boom years of the 1980s put the limited space under severe pressure. Thus the essence of Rogers' design was an arrangement to allow for any foreseeable growth to be accommodated over the coming fifty years, while still maintaining a single-volume underwriting room, and at the same time, as has actually happened, to be able to respond to a shrinkage in the space needed.

The centre of the building is a twelve-storey-high barrel-vaulted glass atrium, around which are rings of office accommodation. The underwriting room is on the principal floor with the lower rings of offices designed to be converted to take any eventual overflow from the main underwriting room as and when required. Around the atrium, which has often been compared to Paxton's Crystal Palace , are six satellite towers containing lifts, services, washrooms and escape stairs. These towers have become highly expressive elements, dominant parts of the overall composition and a measure of Rogers' predilection for Louis Kahn's concept of served and servant spaces. Rogers explains this division as follows: 'Whereas the framework of the building has a long life expectancy, the servant areas filled with mechanical equipment have an extremely short life, especially in this energy critical period.'

Rogers' original scheme for the structure, developed with the engineers at Ove Arup and Partners who also worked on the Hong Kong and Shanghai Bank, was a tubular steel system, which would have been fire-proofed by the simple expedient of filling it with water. In the event it would have taken too long to secure the statutory approvals, so a refined concrete structure was adopted instead. The beautifully made concrete stands in contrast to the steel-faced services towers.

Rogers describes the building with the same Meccano set analogy that he once used for the Pompidou, seeing Lloyd's almost as a piece of machinery, a flexible kit of moving parts that is continually changing. 'The key to this juxtaposition of parts is the legibility of the role of each technological component which is functionally stressed to the full,' he says. 'Thus one may recognise in each part its process of manufacture, erection, maintenance and finally demolition; the how, why and what of the building. Each single element is isolated and used to give order. Nothing is hidden, everything is expressed. The legibility of the parts gives the building scale, grain and shadow.' But

Just as impressive as the overall conception of Lloyd's is the extraordinary level of inventiveness that has been lavished on every detail, *opposite*, from the humblest aluminium extrusion on escape stairs to the steel assemblies bracing the exterior glazing.

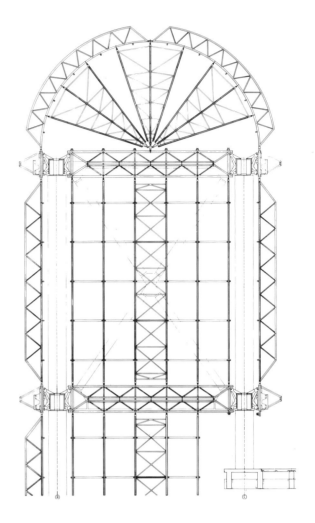

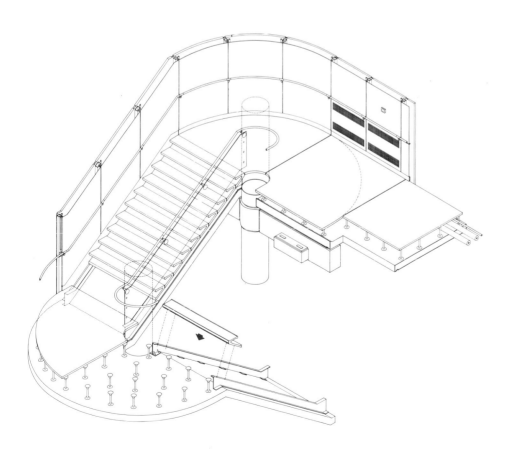

From the Lutine Bell, at the centre of the Room, *this page*, to its close relationship with neighbouring Leadenhall Market, *opposite*, Lloyd's is an intriguing mixture of tradition with the aggressively modern.

beyond the technological symbolism of the towers, they are used to make the most important gesture toward the city setting. The towers are an attempt to match the scale of the bland existing blocks all around the Lloyd's site, but at the same time are of an irregularity that attempts to recognise the altogether more domestic scale of the streets and alleys that still survive from the City's medieval past.

It is no secret that as work progressed on the Lloyd's building, some supporters began to experience doubts. Architectural journalist Martin Pawley compared the external ducting for the air-conditioning system on either side of the atrium walls to a motorcycle engine. And the City of London's planning committee – some of whose members took to calling Lloyd's hideous – were at one time disposed to revoke their planning consents on account of the variation between the original drawings of the project submitted to them and the completed building. The most conspicuous variation was the burgeoning provision of plant rooms atop the service towers.

In his introduction to a monograph on the Rogers office, Peter Cook concluded by expressing himself 'delighted that Rogers work is now achieving a level of uncomfortableness for the general level English architect that one noticed with Stirling's work ten years earlier. They have to admit that it is good, but could they bring themselves to do it, even if they had the talent?'

There is no doubt that there are things about Lloyd's which are uncomfortable. From the south, the building is densely packed with visual information. Pedestrians emerging from Leadenhall Market are confronted with an array of structural servicing and glazing systems each demanding attention. Yet for all Quinlan Terry's appeals to tradition, his notorious Richmond riverside scheme is in fact far less traditional than Lloyd's. For while it is built in an apparently ruthlessly contemporary manner, with a maximum of technological imagery, and seems to represent the very antithesis of tradition, Lloyd's is actually a building in which tradition is very important. It is tailor-made for the insurance brokers of London who have worked in this part of the city for 300 years. It is a Savile Row suit, even if the cut is eccentric. Terry's scheme, despite the apparently familiar character of its brick and stone façades and its slate and tile roofs, is actually the product of a highly contemporary brief, to design speculative offices on an out-of-town site, for an unknown tenant. Ready to wear, rather than made to measure. The exterior plumbing at Lloyd's has given Rogers the chance to create a broken up picturesque silhouette that is less of a disruption to the twisting lanes that form the City fabric than the simple-minded 1960s slabs all around. Unlike the revivalists, Rogers believes that a contemporary vocabulary of materials and forms can still be an appropriate way of building within the city.

The visual complexity of
Lloyd's comes from the
elaboration with which every
element, both structural
and mechanical, is expressed
on the façade, and the refusal
of the architects to take
anything for granted.
Hence the glass box of the
external lifts, *opposite*,
and the prefabricated
lavatory capsules, *below*.

A measure of technology

Architecture is a continuing process of discovery and research. It depends on the gradual refinement of creative ideas and the development of expertise that emerges through time as the starting point for further innovation. Architectural careers that have the stamina to last cannot be be based only on one or two prodigious feats. Rather they are measured by the establishment of a creative repertoire; on the working through of a range of both ideas and architectural techniques that can be deployed in a variety of different contexts. In architecture, perhaps more than in any other comparable creative process, experience is of critical importance. The exploration of ideas, and their testing and development, is something that can only happen over a considerable period of time.

Looking at the work of the Richard Rogers Partnership, it is possible to identify a range of ideas and themes that recur in certain series of buildings which together make up a specific phase of its output. These then give way to other themes, and sometimes reappear much later, or else mutate into new combinations. In the earliest days of Team 4, skylit interiors and complex cross-sections stepping down steep sloping sites constituted one such theme. It was an approach that offered an effective means of dealing with sites that were rarely flat or simple, and a way of introducing a relationship with the natural environment into architecture. With it came a vocabulary for the use of a certain palette of materials, some of which have remained with Rogers throughout his career. Look, for example, at the kitchen layout in the house that Team 4 designed for the Creek Vean house at the start of the 1960s, and Rogers' own kitchen in the house in Chelsea that he built a quarter of a century later; in both you will find a freestanding stainless steel island, an apparently functional artefact that is also a totem, an object which celebrates the mundane functions of domestic life. The basic form entirely transcends the pragmatic changes that have transformed the actual

Designed for an out-of-town site on the edge of Nantes, *left*, Usines Center at St Herblain (1986) is a highly visible shopping centre with a refinement in its details that is rare in this building type. The cable-supported roof and vivid colours make it a local landmark.

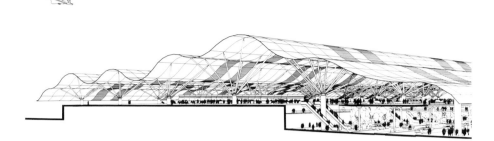

domestic fittings needing to be accommodated, from the primitive waste disposal units of 1962 to their slick and over-engineered late 1980s equivalents. Equally, the sparse aesthetic of block walls, window openings with invisible frames and glass doors with handles planted directly on to the glass with no obvious visible means of support, established a certain approach to dealing with the problems of detail that have preoccupied all architects, while leaving enough room to consider the rather more critical notions of scale, elevation and form. After all, the details can take care of themselves once you have established a basic approach.

The early domestic projects were followed by a series of industrial buildings that have their roots in the Reliance Controls factory built on the edge of Swindon by Team 4. It is a series which includes the B&B furniture company's buildings outside Como (a Piano and Rogers project); the UOP Fragrances factory in Surrey; and the PA Technology laboratory in Cambridge. While these use different cladding materials – sometimes profiled metal, brightly coloured fibreglass, or glass-reinforced cement – these too have a certain commonality of approach. They are all the product of an era in which the architectural profession was faced with a new kind of commission. Bright, youngish entrepreneurs anxious to make their mark, and with a genuine belief in the need to reflect their progressive aspirations in their buildings, were looking to bright, progressive young architects to design their factories and offices. But even these skin buildings always showed a preference for legibility, for making clear the underlying essence of the building structure, a move that is in sharp contrast to the outwardly similar output of Norman Foster at the same time, which was much more to do with the creation of buildings with skins that were like taut membranes. Typically, a Rogers design would express joints between panels clearly, and would show how cladding was held in position and supported by the structure. Foster, meanwhile, would attempt to make them all invisible and entirely seamless.

A new series of designs can be seen as having its starting point in the Fleetguard factory in Brittany, designed in 1979, a building which celebrated structure in a way that was different from anything that had gone before. In order to free the production line floor from fixed columns as much as possible, the building used a cable-supported mast structure to support the roof. The theory was that this would allow for a simple reconfiguration of the production floor without the owner's room for manoeuvre being limited by structural constraints. But it also had the effect of establishing a new architectural type which was later taken up by others, including Norman Foster with his design for Renault's factory in Swindon, and by Nick Grimshaw for his ice-rink in Oxford. The basic industrial shed was given a distinctive identity by piercing its skin with a mast structure, providing an escape route from the over-simplified box. This

Early studies for the giant new Terminal Five at London's Heathrow Airport, *above,* **produced the idea of a continuous undulating roof that would have had the impact of a range of low rolling hills. A similar theme was used in designs for the Liverpool Olympic arena.**

The practice completed two major buildings in 1994: the new headquarters for Channel 4 television, *below*, and the European Court of Human Rights at Strasbourg, *middle and bottom*. Both buildings employ distinctive circular forms.

sequence of industrial buildings provided a chance for Rogers to realise in a practical form some of the ideas underlying his earlier work. The idea of the building as a machine, one that was put together like a car, in which the idea of architecture as a composition seemed like an irrelevance in the face of the exigencies of production, and in which vivid colour and strong structural form said everything, was realised in this series of buildings that literally took on the characteristics of machines.

Of the partnership's buildings, the 1982 Inmos microprocessor plant in Newport, and the PA Technology laboratory in Princeton, designed around the same time, also follow this pattern. Inmos, with its steel containers hoisted up on to its roof, and each numbered and linked by a mass of cables and pipes, looks as if it could literally move. The image is of some giant dockside travelling crane. The initial studies, which placed even more servicing on the roof, were more memorable still – not a crane but a starship. The shopping centre in Nantes (1986) is even closer to the Fleetguard factory in the shape of its forest of steel masts piercing through its roof. It came about as a commission from a client who was so taken by the Fleetguard building that he had asked another architect to copy it for one of his own buildings, an out-of-town shopping shed close to Paris's Charles de Gaulle Airport. This dubious tribute took the form of a standard industrial box, decorated with a superfluous maypole steel mast festooned with purely symbolic steel cables. Faced with the less-than-satisfactory result, the client decided that the original was infinitely more convincing and went to the Rogers Partnership to build the Usines Center in Nantes.

For Rogers, this was a chance to come to terms with the most universal new building type of the 1980s, the retail shopping shed. The idea was of a low-budget out-of-town building with costs pared to the minimum to support a pile 'em high, sell 'em cheap retailing operation. The sense of identity that the architecture provides helps to civilise

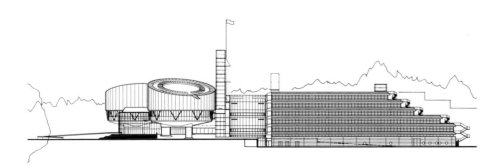

the brutality of the basic idea. The partnership brought an eye-searing colour scheme to the Nantes project, and a sharply observed and detailed transformation of the basic vocabulary of materials.

Another strand to Rogers' work is the expressionism of semi-detached towers containing circulation stairs that has its roots in Coin Street and Lloyd's, and which came to the fore in the unbuilt design for the Whittington Avenue development in the City of London, in the Seattle high-rise, and in the Farnborough air terminal. So far it has only been realised as a secondary element at Lloyd's, and at the Channel 4 headquarters in London, but it is nonetheless an essential part of the practice's belief in the potential of giving buildings legibility and scale by breaking them up into their constituent parts. The daunting effect of a huge box is softened if you can easily tell from the outside where the entry and exit points are: when the stair towers are pushed out of the envelope on to the exterior, it becomes clear where you go in and where you come out. The partnership also uses toilets, service towers and lifts to similar ends. It creates open flexible interior spaces from which all the fixed elements have been removed to be located on the edges. In a sense it is decorative, as the mundane essentials are exposed and dissected, providing a contemporary equivalent to the sense of scale and detail that comes from the purely decorative addition of classical detail. And it could be seen as a paradoxical use of technology for manneristic ends. But more importantly, it is an attempt to make a building more legible and understandable, and therefore less threatening and alienating. For those who understand the signals, the building is explaining how it is made and what it does.

Following on from this phase is the series of wave-roofed buildings that began with the competition-winning design for Heathrow's fifth terminal, one which may itself have learnt something from the winning design by Renzo Piano that Rogers backed as a judge in the Kansai Airport competition. It re-emerged as a form for the design for the Olympic arena in Liverpool's docklands, which made up part of Britain's unsuccessful bid for the Olympic Games for the year 2000. Unlike the string of earlier industrial buildings, represented by Fleetguard and PA Technology in America, it is not the masts which give these buildings shape, but the roof itself, as it soars up and over the structural supports like a breaking wave, rather than allowing those supports to puncture it.

The early 1990s will see the completion of two major new buildings by the partnership – the European Court of Human Rights in Strasbourg and the headquarters for the British television station Channel 4 in London – and each represents a fresh departure. At Strasbourg, Rogers has come closest to building the kind of revived Mendelsohn, early modernist structure that he has examined in such other designs as the aborted project for a new office building at Whittington Avenue next to the Lloyd's building, and which also left its trace on the National Gallery extension scheme. Without any nostalgic attempt to recall specific historical memory, the partnership has designed a complex which, geometrically based as it is and with its curves, inevitably recalls the shapes and forms of Mendelsohn.

The most recent projects show an ever wider spread of approaches. The definition of one of the partnership's buildings now ranges from the glass pavilions of the Lloyd's Register building at Liphook, dropped in the landscape like railway coaches, to the Bordeaux courthouse extension, which aims to knit itself into the historic fabric of the city, while still providing a measure of architectural drama inside. It is equally represented by the soaring wedge of glass that is the, as yet unbuilt, London headquarters for the Japanese bank Daiwa on London Wall, and the studies for prefabricated high-rise housing towers in Korea. Then there are the partnership's Japanese projects, which constitute another distinct group of designs. In Tokyo, a city that looks like the one in *Blade Runner* brought to life, there are few buildings that enjoy the luxury of an unencumbered site. The streets appear as a mass of façades, shrieking for individual attention but united by their very stridency, which somehow merge into a single blur of neon and glass. To describe the ever-present overhead power cables, the disorientating juxtapositions of scale, or the outlandish forms studded with giant outdoor television screens as ugly is meaningless. They simply create a setting in which the most chaste and austere minimalism coexists with dreary banality, and in which one is apparently totally oblivious to the other – or even impossible without the other.

Tokyo doesn't look anything like the traditional idea of the western city. With its dense mix of uses, its packed pedestrian streets, and its elaborate department stores, it is closer to the Victorian metropolis than it is to the centreless web of freeways, business parks and rotting downtowns that constitute most American and many

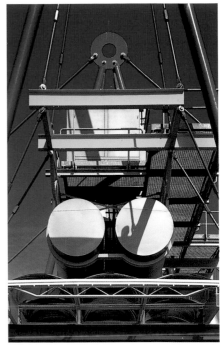

The Fleetguard factory at Quimper in Brittany, *opposite page, bottom*, completed in 1979, was the first in what turned out to be a series of Rogers buildings that use mast-supported roof structures, partly for practical reasons, to produce uninterrupted interiors, but also to give some sense of identity to what would otherwise have been bland and anonymous industrial structures. It was the clarity and elegance of the Fleetguard structure that attracted Rogers' client for the Nantes shopping centre, *left and right*. In Princeton, the PA Technology laboratory, *opposite page, top, and this page, top*, uses a different structural system. The roof is cantilevered from the central corridor, with cables from the A frame used to reduce the load. It is a system similar to the one used for the Inmos microprocessor factory at Newport, which allows the laboratories to be free of intrusive columns permitting future changes in working processes, and also means the high proportion of the necessary servicing can be carried outside the building envelope, where it can be easily reached for maintenance.

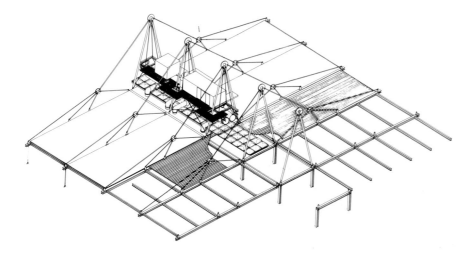

The PA Technology structure at Princeton, *above*, reduces the number of internal columns to a minimum – just two central rows defining a circulation route. The shopping building in Nantes, *opposite page*, has to deal with larger spans, two storeys, and a very different pattern of use. The mast structure is arranged to allow for shop units on either side of a central mall.

European cities. If any one – let alone all – of the projects that the Richard Rogers Partnership has worked on in Tokyo were to be built in London, they would create an architectural sensation. Even in the setting of the Japanese capital, their structural virtuosity and flamboyant design can hardly be said to merge into the background, but their impact is entirely different. In London they would be regarded as provocative, but in the context of Tokyo, where very inch of space gained through the manipulation of planning controls is a precious commodity, they can be seen as attempts to civilise the development process since they do rather more than simply package space efficiently. The economics of development in Tokyo, with its very high land costs, dictate that all new building, including high-profile landmarks designed by western architects, have to be planned to extract the very last millimetre of floor space from the density regulations. By bringing the view of an outsider to the problem, the Rogers partnership has managed to address the constraints of the system in a fresh way.

Much new building in Japan is closer to product design than architecture. The competence and organisation of Japanese contractors, along with the skills of component suppliers, allow architects working there to rely on off-the-shelf skins for their designs that have the sleek gloss of a brand new Lexus. The sophisticated exteriors, however, often conceal architecturally vapid buildings. So far, this seems to have suited the developers who, as in every other country, prefer a trouble-free construction process. But the position is now beginning to change, not least because of the large number of western architects being imported to work in Japan. This is not the first time that Japan has made extensive use of western architects: Europeans played a significant part in the building of Tokyo during the Meiji period in the 1870s, when the Japanese elite, fearful of suffering the same fate as China at the hands of the western powers, embarked on a breakneck industrialisation programme. The Englishman Josiah Conder was responsible for building western-style red brick terraces in the Ginza area of the city. He was joined by a number of lesser known designers who gave Japan railway stations, post offices and other symbols of modernisation, and paved the way for Frank Lloyd Wright's Imperial Hotel. For more than twenty years after the Second World War, however, with the exception of Le Corbusier's Museum of Modern Art which opened in 1959, western architects working in Japan were largely confined to diplomatic compounds and expo sites. The situation changed again in the mid-1980s, when the soaring yen suddenly made western imports, including architects, seem cheap. As a result, everybody from Philippe Starck to Christopher Alexander, by way of Mario Botta, Norman Foster and Michael Graves, has built in Japan. The reasons for this phenomenon are complex. Partly, it is the result of a strategic decision taken by the Japanese government, as part of the price of fending off tariff barriers in America and Europe. But also, along with foreign cars,

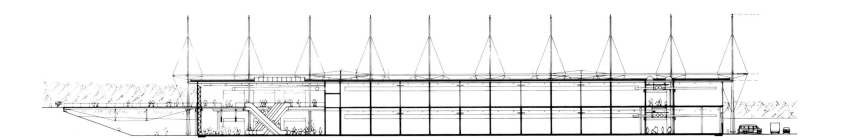

French wine and Italian clothes, exotic architects became fashionable.

Japan, of course, is far from being the first society to import architectural talent on a major scale, but it must be the first to have done so where there has been no practical need. Despite substantial cultural linguistic and cost barriers, western architects are flown half way around the globe not because they can do things that are technically better than the country's own designers, but because they can do things differently. Japan offers a hot-house environment, one which is forcing the pace of architectural change. And it has the resources and the opportunities to attract the most significant architects from around the world, as was indicated by the 1989 competition to design the Tokyo Forum, a multi-purpose cultural and convention centre on the site of the old city hall, that city is becoming a place in which architectural attitudes are now defined. Rogers, along with James Stirling and dozens of other well known designers, entered the Tokyo Forum competition. His entry was a striking design with an exposed structural frame supporting three auditoria expressed as steel-plated capsules suspended from the top of the frame. It would have stood comparison with the Pompidou and Lloyd's as being among his most significant works. In the event it did not win, but was a sign of the event's importance.

Working in Japan presents a serious dilemma for western architects. They are confronted with a context in which a complete lack of aesthetic control on development has created an undeniably exhilarating visual chaos. Architects are often expected to justify their presence by doing something even more surprising and astonishing than what is there already. Yet in Tokyo, they are in a city which it is impossible to upstage architecturally and which, despite the apparent visual anarchy, is in fact tightly restricted by the technical demands of density, daylight, and anti-earthquake and typhoon building codes. What they can do, however, is attempt

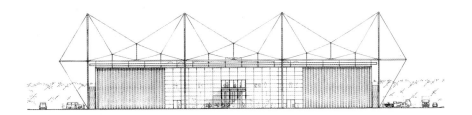

Richard Rogers | **A measure of technology**

Designed to register at the scale of the motorway city as much as the pedestrian, the Nantes shopping centre, *preceding pages, above, right and opposite*, transforms the humblest of building types. The strong colours and exposed ductwork of the Pompidou Centre had become the inspiration for a whole school of commercialised high-tech. Here the Rogers office, which had invented the look, for once found itself called upon to apply it.

The Inmos factory, *this page and opposite*, was built with government money as a high-profile investment in advanced technology in Britain. The choice of architect was a deliberate signal of the intention of the company's founder Iain Barron – who had earlier commissioned an inflatable laboratory from Norman Foster – to build a showcase. Public money meant that the site of the plant was shifted from Bristol to Newport, and a deliberate attempt was made to source components, such as the cladding, locally. The company went through a variety of incarnations and was sold and resold, reflecting the changing fortunes of the industry.

Richard Rogers I A measure of technology

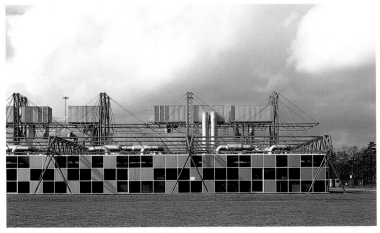

While the partnership worked on a whole range of planning studies for sites in London's Docklands, the only big project to be realised was the Reuters Data Centre, *above* until the Channel Four building in Westminster *pages101-102*. In a belated attempt to atone for the architectural anarchy over which it had presided, the London Docklands Development Corporation commissioned two pumping stations, one of them from Rogers, *overleaf*.
Like Inmos, the Linn factory in Glasgow, *opposite*, completed in 1987, was the product of the determination of an entrepreneur to build a plant that would be a visible symbol of a commitment to high quality manufacturing, in this case audio components.

to change the way in which buildings are designed and made. While many westerners working in Japan were content to rely on occasional flying visits, in 1987 the Richard Rogers Partnership established an office in Tokyo.

The partnership brought the same improvisational methods to the construction of its Japanese projects that it has used elsewhere, and applied them in a context free of the aesthetic control that has had such an impact in Britain. The result could be seen as a luxuriant new phase for the firm, as if a plant species, conditioned to a harsh climate and clinging to rocks for survival suddenly found itself transplanted to the tropics. Nevertheless, working in Japan brings its own strict controls and limitations, such as the restrictions on height, floor area and building profile, generated by density and daylight regulations in Tokyo. Daylight controls can be particularly complicated, determined in some cases by shadow projection, and in others by light cones. In almost every case, the shape of the partnership's designs for buildings in Tokyo is a close reflection of the permissible envelope indicated by the interpretation of these regulations. Despite the diversity of Tokyo's streetlife, there are also strict zoning rules which usually take the form of limiting commercial development beyond a certain distance from a major road. In effect this tends to mean height limits, rather than user restrictions. At the same time, development sites are almost always shaped by the nature of Japanese attitudes to the holding of land. Plot sizes are often very small – there are new office buildings in the Ginza that are just two metres wide. Outright sales of land are rare and sites are often traded between owners to create workable building plots.

If land arrangements in Tokyo are distinctive, so is the construction process. The Japanese way of building is very different from the British system. The contractor takes responsibility for the performance of a building and is responsible for detailing the design. It is according to his drawings that the building is constructed. So while building sites are immaculately well organised and spotlessly clean, there is great opposition to using untested technical solutions and non-standard components. There is, for example, no tradition of architectural steelwork in Japan. In Britain, by contrast, while the general approach on site and the overall quality of organisation may be less efficient than in Japan, there is still a network of small artisan fabricators capable of producing high quality components to the direct specifications of the architect, and installing them on site. There is a parallel in the car industry where, despite Britain's struggle to match Japanese standards of mass production, at the level of high-performance racing cars, British manufacturers still enjoy a considerable lead.

The effect of all this is to limit the chances of producing refined, delicate structures. Instead, the Japanese approach has been to design simple but robust frames that are massive and sometimes over-designed, rather than tailored to reflect the actual

The practice moved into new riverside offices in Hammersmith during the 1980s. The development included the conversion of a series of light industrial buildings into studios, and the construction of a terrace of apartments on the adjoining site, *opposite page*. At the same time Rogers himself was working on the conversion of two adjoining terraced houses in Chelsea into a new home. The centrepiece is a huge double-height space, *this page*, with a mezzanine that clearly shows the lasting impact on Rogers of Chareau's Maison de Verre.

A study, *below*, for a
landmark structure for the
centre of Lyons for GRC, the
company that built the
Rogers-designed shopping
centre in Nantes. The tower,
which would have served
a complex of offices and
apartments, has similarities
with the design of the
National Gallery extension,
and suggests a continuing
interest in the expressionist
modernism of Erich
Mendelsohn.

distribution of forces. Following all the codes, which insist on minimum dimensions rather than performance specifications, can mean that structural steel is considerably larger than comparable structural members are in less exposed parts of the world. The problem faced by Rogers is the tendency all this has to produce buildings that are almost cartoon versions of his intentions. Patience and mutual confidence, which is slowly and painstakingly established between clients, architects, contractors and suppliers, are necessary to avoid this. One of the first major structures to be designed – the Iikura development – was among the first proposed in Tokyo to use an exposed steel structure with no applied fire protection. The authorities had to be satisfied that a combination of intumescent paint protection and the use of a new fire-rated steel will provide adequate safety levels.

Failing to win the Forum competition has meant that Rogers' initial buildings in Japan are, for the most part, modest in scale and utilitarian in their range of uses. Within a relatively small floor area, they will contain a mixture of offices, showrooms, retail outlets and restaurants. While this building type is familiar in Tokyo, the way in which the architect has determinedly sought to shape not just the overall form but the way in which the building is put together will seem quite strange. The partnership is attempting to make buildings which can hold their own in Tokyo, without losing their essential qualities. For what is really at stake here is the definition of architecture: whether it is simply a matter of signs and outward appearances; or whether – in the context of Tokyo where nothing is permanent and where a building can adopt any visual language one might choose – it is possible to give it substance, too. Such substance can only come when buildings are designed with strong internal consistency. Structure and detail need to have the same level of refinement as the skin if the building itself is going to work as architecture rather than scenery.

When Tokyo's city government took the decision to abandon its Kenzo Tange-designed 1950s building near the Imperial Palace and follow the drift westward of the city's population to a massive new twin tower City Hall at Shinjuku, also designed by Tange, this time in a queasy gothic manner, it left open the question of what to do with the site. It is one of the most valuable plots of land in the world – at the height of the 1980s property boom, a regularly repeated statistic was that a few acres of land in Tokyo's primary business district, Marounuchi, were worth enough to buy the whole of California. Such is the area's desirability for Japanese financial institutions, that even the tiniest plots of land here are sought after. They rarely come on to the open market, and there are long waiting lists for those that do. A site as large as this one is unique, and could have commanded almost any price.

A generation ago, when Tokyo was busy obliterating its natural topography by running motorways on stilts along its rivers, the temptation to turn the site over to commercial redevelopment might well have proved irresistible. It is a measure of the shifting nature of the Japanese view of the city that this did not happen and is also evidence that the idea of civic responsibility had begun to take a stronger hold. The solution eventually adopted was to build a massive complex of public halls, to be used for conventions and performances – the aforementioned Tokyo Forum. It was intended as something between the Lincoln Center and the Westminster Conference Centre. Its design was the subject of an international architectural competition, one of the largest Japan has seen. Attracting hundreds of entries, it was eventually won by the New York-based, Argentine-born Rafael Vinoly. Rogers, working with Mitsubishi's construction arm, took the idea of the forum literally. Very much in the tradition of the Pompidou, the aim was to create a public space that would act as a magnet for people. To that end, the three principal auditoria would be hoisted up off the ground and suspended from a giant steel cradle, leaving the ground underneath as an open amphitheatre, formed by the roof of an exhibition hall buried in the basement. This would have been one of the most transparent of Rogers' buildings, putting on show not just air-conditioning ducts and lifts, but the very essence of the building. Instead of partially dissecting the elevations, there would be no façades at all. Rather the building would have consisted of nothing more than an expressed structure, and suspended capsules housing the auditoria. The metaphor adopted by the Rogers team working on the project to describe the scheme was that of a dry dock with three ship hulls suspended in a protective cradle. The auditoria would have been faced with steel plate, just as if they were huge ocean-going liners. Huge institutional structures of this kind tend to be dominated by blank, windowless walls, providing a forbidding and anonymous exterior. The partnership's strategy was to avoid this as much as possible by making the building's parts explicit. The provision of facilities encouraging a wide range of social

The first of the partnership's German projects, the Zoofenster tower, *below*, predated its planning studies for the crucial sites between the old eastern and western halves of Berlin.
The fluctuations of the Japanese property market brought western architects to the country when it boomed, but left a number of projects, such as the Iikura building, stranded when it evaporated. However, the more modest Kabuki-cho building, *opposite*, also in Tokyo and combining restaurants and shops with offices, was finally completed in 1993.
The Tokyo Forum submission, *overleaf*, showed more clearly what the firm was capable of.

activities in and around the building would have blurred the distinction between inside and outside, and created an open and inviting complex, rather than a blank, and intimidating one.

Of all the Japanese projects, this is perhaps the most significant, and not just because it is the largest. Had it been built, it would have stood alongside the Pompidou and Lloyd's as a major signpost in the shifting concerns of the partnership. After Lloyd's it looked for a while as though a particular line of architectural enquiry had reached a natural limit. There was nowhere further to take the idea of served and servant space. Further buildings in the same idiom would simply be improvising on themes that had already been well worked out. The Rogers office began to move instead towards an exploration of the expressive possibilities of an architectural language derived from Erich Mendelsohn, but the Tokyo Forum looked like a return to the ideas set out in the Pompidou and their further development. As an architectural object, the project would have had its biggest impact on the side walls, with the three primary auditoria projecting forward from the shelter of the portal frames, reflecting their varying sizes. The rake of the auditorium floor would have been reflected in the form of the capsule slung from the portal frame, with the entrances from the top calling for a network of snaking escalator tubes to carry audiences up from the Forum floor. Tokyo has the teeming street life and the organisation to use such a space to the full.

While the Tokyo office continues to work on a range of projects, the partnership has also established an office in Berlin where it is working on a high-rise tower in what was the western half of the city close to the Zoo station, and is involved with a number of masterplanning projects. It is also busy in Korea and China. But it is in France that it has done most of its European work, with an airport in Marseilles, its competition-winning design for law courts in Bordeaux, urban design studies in Nice and around Paris, and a number of projects for high-rise towers in Lyons .

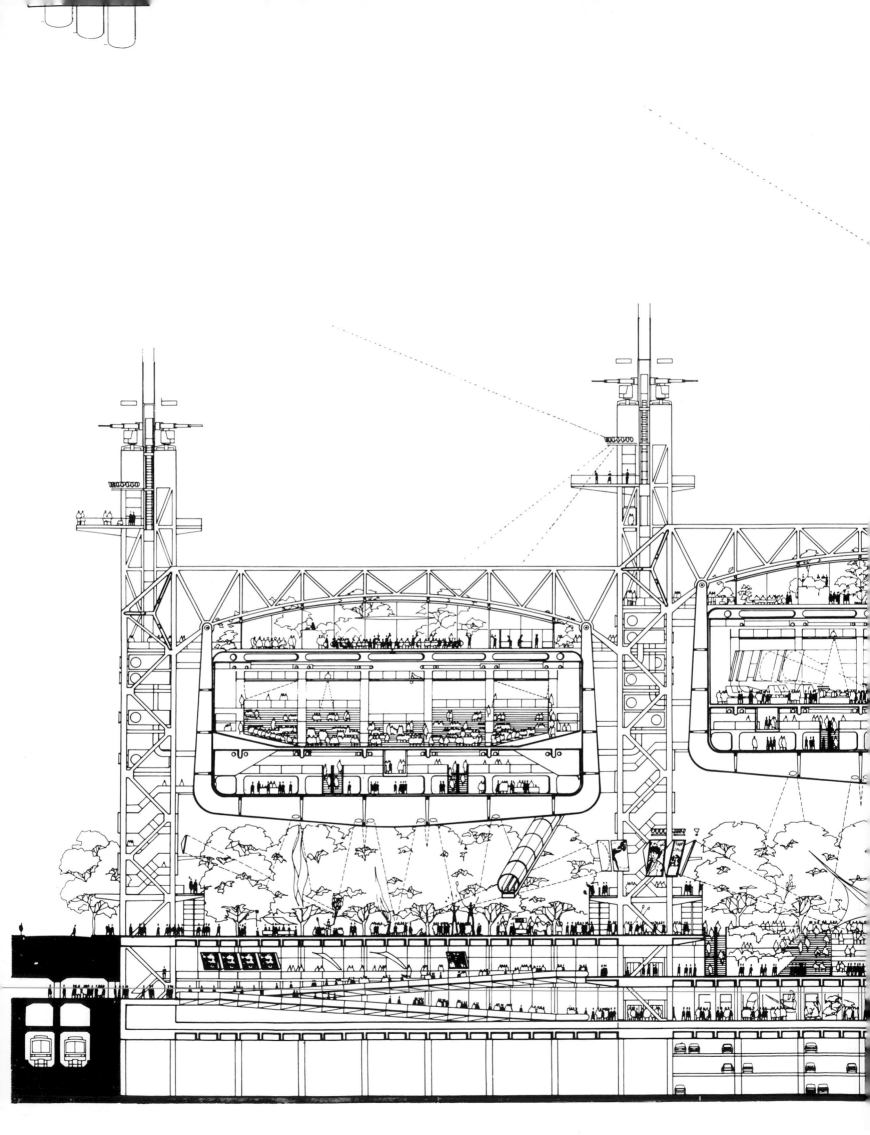

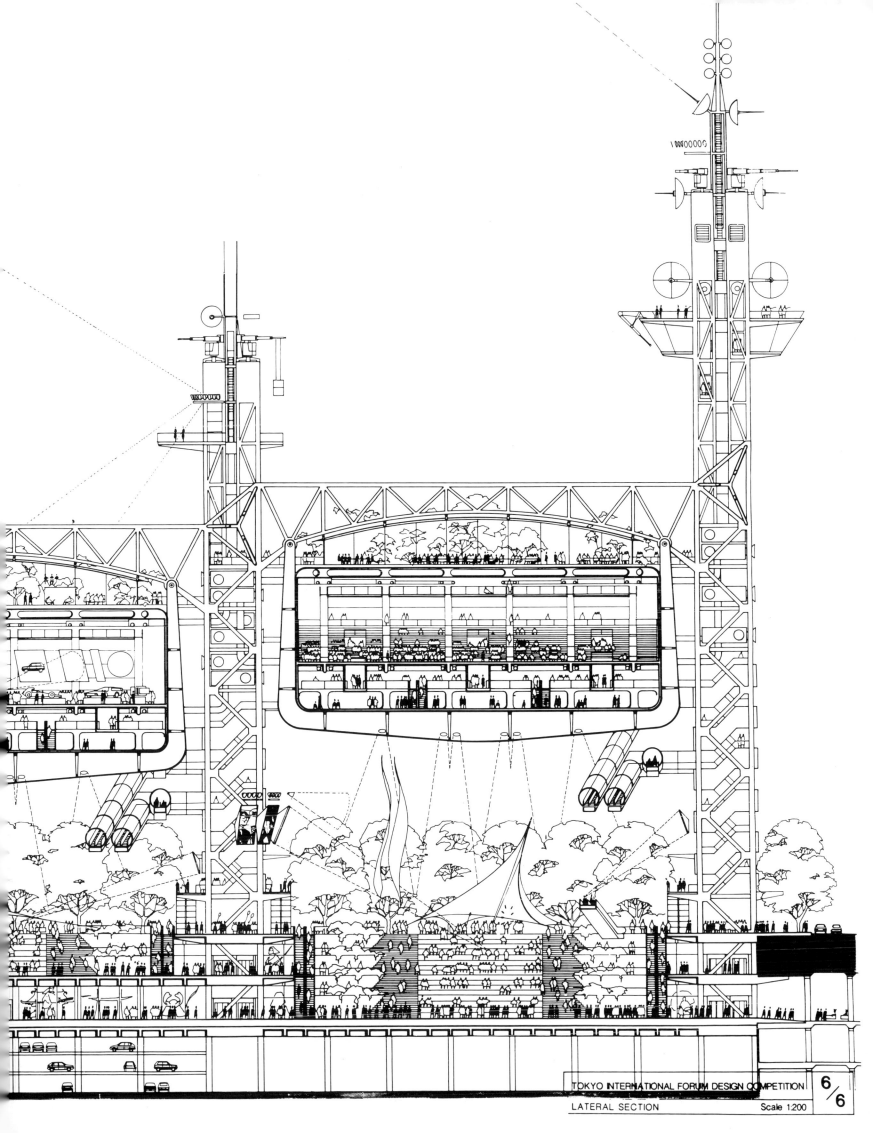

TOKYO INTERNATIONAL FORUM DESIGN COMPETITION

LATERAL SECTION

Scale 1:200

6/6

France has continued to be important to Rogers. The Court of Human Rights in Strasbourg, *opposite*, opens in 1994. Marseilles Airport's new terminal, *left and below*, is the first stage of Rogers work there. And in 1992 the partnership won a commission to build a court complex in Bordeaux (*not shown*).

5 Rebuilding the city

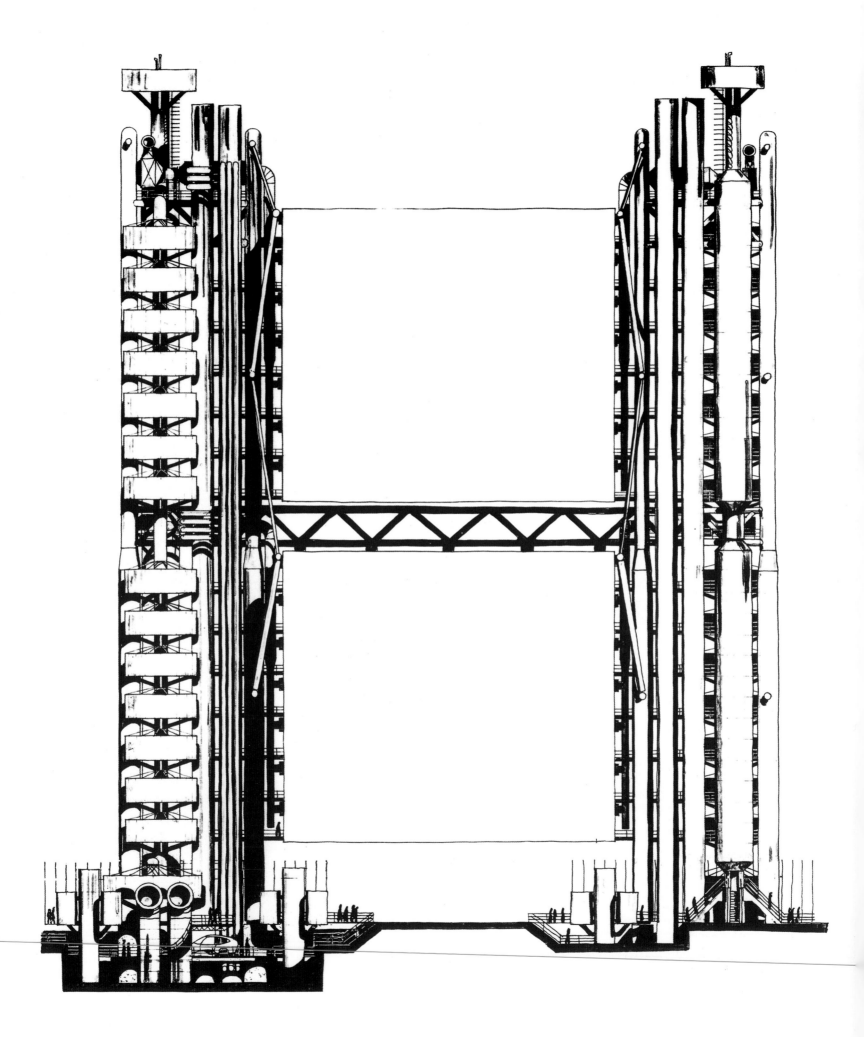

If architecture went through a difficult period in the 1970s and 1980s, urbanism fared still worse at the hands of its critics. The violent reaction to the legacy of the recent past focused in that period on the impact it had had on the character and grain of the city more than on the alleged shortcomings of individual buildings. In less than a generation, all the prescriptions for rescuing the industrial city from decay and squalor that had been advanced with so much confidence and optimism by Modern Movement planners were seen not as solutions but as disastrous mistakes, interventions that had made things worse not better. The received wisdom for building new settlements had come to be seen as socially arid and aesthetically impoverished.

The object-in-the-park school of planning, functional zoning and high-rise housing were all subjects of furious attack. As a result city planning, from having been treated as an essentially positive process, designed to make things happen, turned into a negative one. The primary objective became the perceived need to stop bad things from happening, rather than encouraging good things. Thus every old building was automatically considered to be superior to every new one. When new buildings were absolutely unavoidable, then the conventional wisdom was that new should be made to resemble the old as closely as possible.

While theoretical planning took on an increasingly abstract character, the physical nature of planning was neglected. The discipline was in danger of atrophying into irrelevance. Yet if the profession had suffered a failure of nerve, the problems of urbanism had not gone away. It was a subject in which Richard Rogers became more and more interested. He rejected the idea that contextual sensitivity always called for architects to mimic the forms of surrounding buildings. And he was equally reluctant to accept that planning could only be a conservative process. Rogers cites such diverse examples as the Piazza de la Signoria in Florence and the Cambridge backs to support

The partnership's studies for the Coin Street site in London concentrated on developing a building form that could accommodate the offices and shops required by the project's developer in such a way that the complex become a part of the urban fabric, rather than remain an isolated object. At ground level the whole development would have been open to the public.

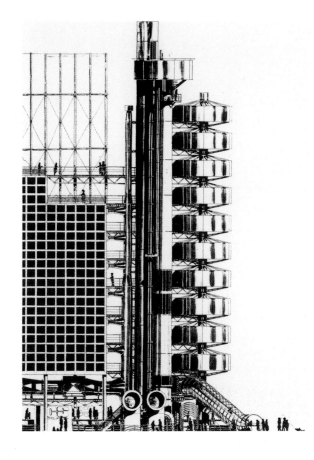

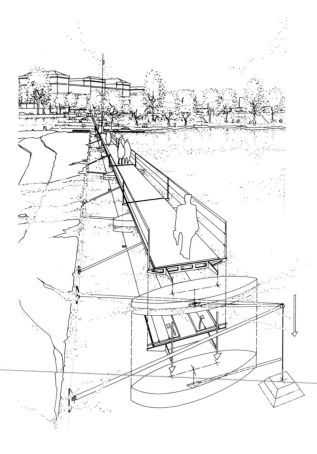

his contention that architectural excellence in very different forms can coexist creatively. Equally, he refused to accept that it was desirable to use architecture as a kind of camouflage – a cosmetic treatment for new building types, applied as a surface layer in a misguided attempt to maintain that nothing had changed in society. In his view, by concentrating on historical styles the critics of modern architecture contrived to ignore the real forces shaping change in the city.

What motivated Rogers even more than the ambition to create visually dynamic cities was to match that with a social dynamism. A city for Rogers is not simply a beautiful object, but is essentially a social mechanism, a place to encourage both the everyday interactions of civilised life, both work and pleasure, as well as the civic formalities. The partnership's attitude towards planning was to see it as a positive force, not simply a conservative or negative one. The Coin Street project on the south bank of the Thames offered an early chance to formulate a more positive approach to redeveloping a largely derelict city centre site. Predictably, Rogers was not satisfied with simply creating an isolated piece of architecture, but was determined not just to give it an appropriate form, but also to make it part of a larger urban project. The partnership saw the chance to create a new route sweeping up from Waterloo Station, enclosed by a galleria formed by two parallel blocks of offices with shops and restaurants at ground level, and culminating in a new pedestrian bridge that would take people across to the other side of the river. It would be a development that, as the architects saw it, would go a long way to help break down the division between the north and south banks of the river. Rogers had equally bold urban intentions for the Lloyd's building, with which he had hoped to echo some of the social success of the Pompidou. The original design envisaged a much greater degree of public interaction with retailing outlets and cafés at ground level, as well as a much more open and accessible architectural form in the context of the bland anonymity of the buildings all around. It was, however, issues of security rather than a negative reaction to the plan from Lloyd's that led to the idea's rejection.

Gradually the partnership found itself addressing a series of other equally taxing urban problems. In Florence there was the strategy it prepared for the banks of the Arno. It was also involved with plans put forward by Fiat to carry out a major redevelopment of the site of one of its redundant factories in the city's suburb of Novoli, although the aesthetic approach was not fixed. In its proposals for remodelling the Royal Opera House in London's Covent Garden, it suggested a historically accurate reconstruction of the façades on to the piazza that had originally been designed by Inigo Jones. The summation of Rogers' thinking on urbanism was the proposal that the partnership put forward as part of the 'Foster, Rogers, Stirling' exhibition at the Royal Academy in 1986. It took the form of a plan for the restructuring of the centre of

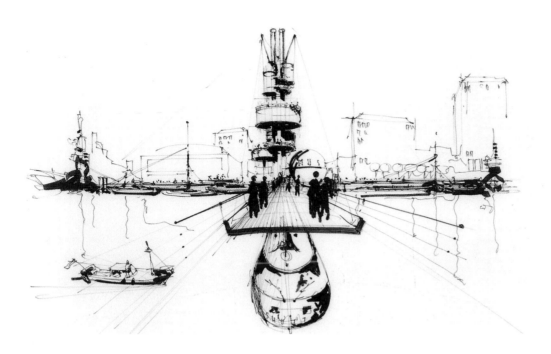

Using new buildings and creating open space within the city to restore the public realm to the pedestrian has been a continuing concern, whether it is in the shape of the public route that would have formed an integral part of the Coin Street blocks, *opposite page, top*, or in the work on a riverside walkway for the Arno in Florence including a submersible pedestrian pontoon, *opposite page, bottom*.
The Rogers project displayed at the 'Foster Rogers Stirling' Royal Academy exhibition in 1986, *left*, also looked at ways of making London a more sympathetic place for the pedestrian user of open spaces, with its plans for a new pedestrian footbridge connecting Waterloo with Whitehall, *below*.

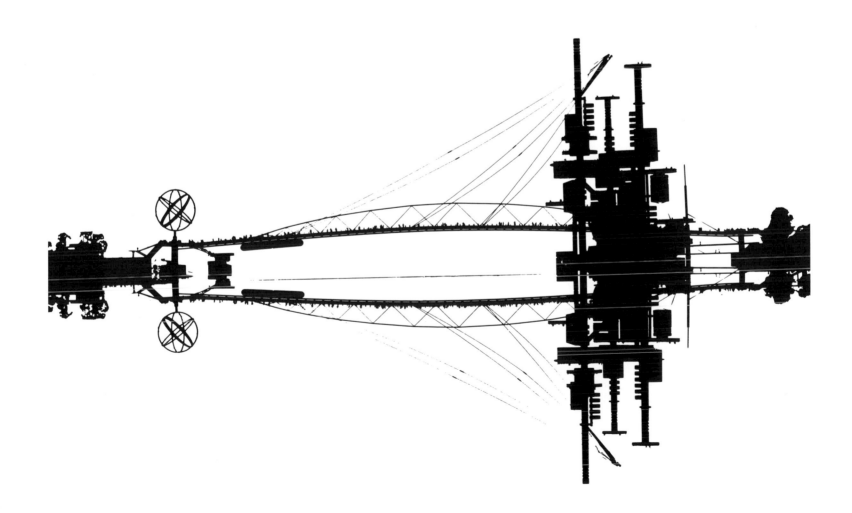

London, and involved the demolition of the existing Hungerford Bridge, and the creation of a spectacular new river crossing. The new bridge would be integrated with a series of floating restaurants and cultural facilities, as well as a people-mover system connecting Waterloo with Trafalgar Square. On the south bank, Rogers proposed a little judicious demolition to open up vistas across the Thames, which would provide passengers arriving on the new cross-Channel railway with an unforgettable view of London. On the north bank, Rogers' most dramatic proposal was to bury the existing road along the Embankment in a tube on the bottom of the Thames so as to remove the heavy traffic that currently divides London from its waterfront.

In Rogers' view, urbanism is a species of surgery, depending on selective demolition and rebuilding to reveal connections and relationships between existing spaces and buildings. But despite this apparent radicalism, his objectives are reassuringly close to the traditional idea of what makes city life convivial. The models of successful urban spaces that Rogers cites are the same as those used by the most traditionalist of architects. They love the centre of Siena, so does Rogers. And just like Leon Krier, Rogers constantly attacks the tendency of cities to become single-function ghettoes, comprising a central business district, in which there are only offices and no people on the streets after five in the evening; residential dormitory suburbs; shopping sheds marooned in car parks; and segregated factory estates. Successful cities, for Rogers, are those that encourage messy diversity, and where many different functions overlap. They are essentially democratic environments, places which allow and inspire people to realise their potential. Where the Richard Rogers Partnership parts company with Krier, or indeed the Prince of Wales, is in the question of the aesthetic treatment of the city, and, most importantly, in his belief that high-rise architecture can have a place in it. In this, Rogers embraces the positive aspects of the modern world.

Floating pontoons in the Thames would have accommodated bars and restaurants and possibly a gallery, linked to both banks by the new footbridge, *left*.

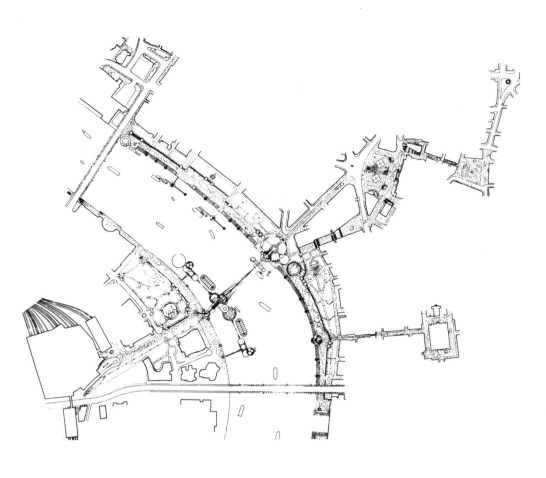

Rogers' Royal Academy scheme proposed reconnecting London with the Thames by sinking the existing busy Embankment road in a tunnel, *opposite, below*. The aim behind the scheme was not to create flamboyant landmarks for their own sake, but to restructure the relationship of one part of the city with another, to provide a dynamic new connection between the forecourt of Waterloo Station – which, with the arrival of Cross Channel trains will become London's European gateway – and Trafalgar Square, *left*.

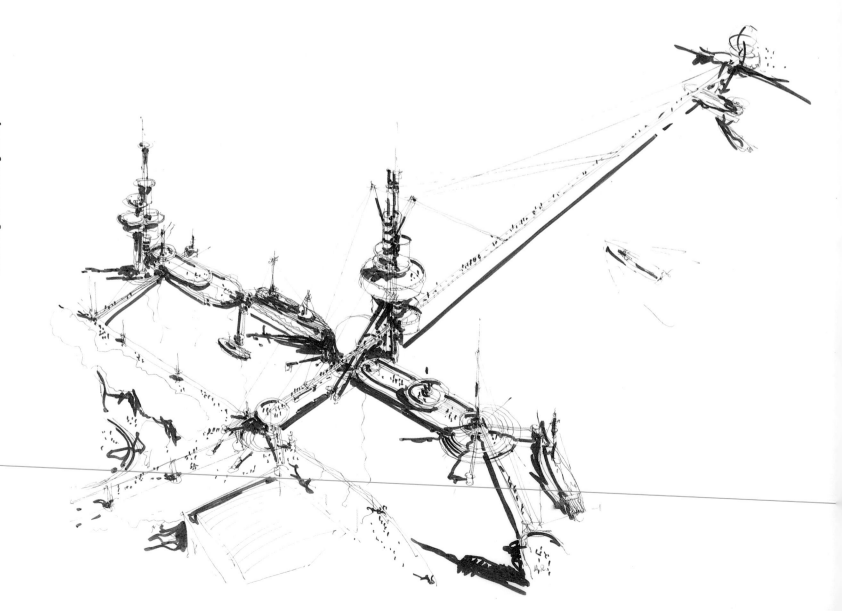

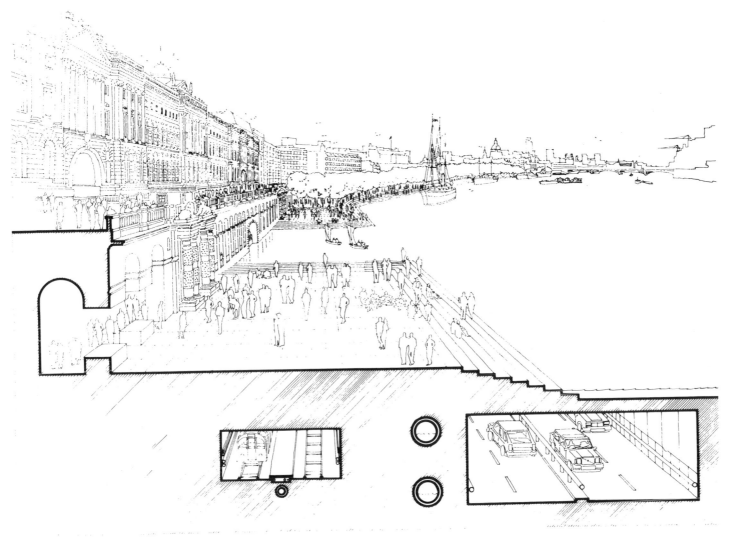

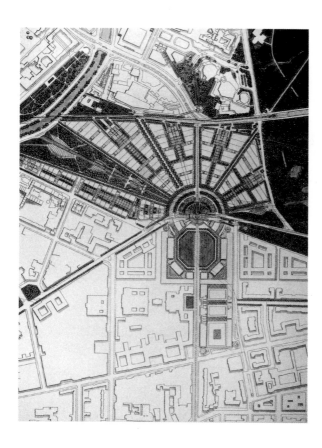

The partnership's studies for the Potsdamer and Leipziger Platz area of Berlin, *above and opposite page*, were an early attempt at restructuring the long-divided city into a united whole. They sought to establish a clearly identifiable urban centre on the site of its old heart that had been demolished both during the war and by the building of the wall. The octagonal open space recreates a historic form obliterated by the wall, while the circus would have been a new focus for the city, allowing for the building of the high-rise landmark structures. Rogers' clients were a consortium of companies who had acquired the site with the intention of building themselves headquarters buildings in the new capital of Germany.

The partnership's urban work is not, of course, confined to Britain, and it is overseas that Rogers has had his most challenging urban commissions. He has had to get to grips not just with the issue of knitting together existing fabric, but has also been closely involved with what will be the crucial new urban centres of the 1990s. In Berlin the partnership has put forward ambitious strategies for the devastated heart of the newly reunited city, where there is a need to sustain the memory of an obliterated urban fabric, to cater to the demands of an international metropolis, and to plan a new slice of the city in a way that minimises energy use. Equally, in a city with the memories and historical resonances of Berlin, it was impossible not to respond to the question of how to shape its future growth without an awareness of the symbolic significance of a newly restored capital. Eventually, Rogers fell foul of the presumption in that town of the necessity to recreate the traditional Berlin courtyard block. Meanwhile, in Shanghai he has worked on one of the exploding new cities of Asia that is now shaping the future of urbanism. As a model for a city, it is entirely different from the European experience, yet it is one that is likely in the future to prove just as significant.

The British have spent so many of the last forty years working on the conviction that their cities have no future and are doomed to dwindle in population and descend into not so gentle squalor, that Rogers' continuing enthusiasm for building the city of tomorrow has had a rough ride. Britain has got so used to the idea of a shrinking future, and the belief that bold plans inevitably turn to dust, that it almost finds decay a comforting prospect. Along with the rest of Europe, it has forgotten what it is like to face up to life in a city in which a population can double and double again in a single lifetime, where a surveyor's grid, laid out with pegs and string in open fields, can mushroom into a skyline of skyscrapers with an urgency that suggests time-lapse photography. It's a daunting as well as an exhilarating prospect, one that demands a quite different psychology from that engendered by a declining or a static city such as London or, for that matter, New York or Paris.

In fact, the British were never quite convinced that they liked the power and vigour of a city in the full flood of growth anyway. Those Victorians who weren't busy building cities were horrified at the shadow cast by the satanic mills and the dangerous freedom they offered the mob. Frantically, they tried to recreate the rural idyll. Perhaps that is why Britain in the age of the Prince of Wales is still hypnotised by a vision of pedestrian squares and Quality Street chocolate-box facades, as if the best it can hope for from the future is to rebuild Dickensian London on the ruins of the 1960s.

Britain went through the explosive growth of the nineteenth century, when Victorian city builders could confidently mortgage the future to build museums, universities, roads, trams, railways and parks, secure that one day there would be twice as many

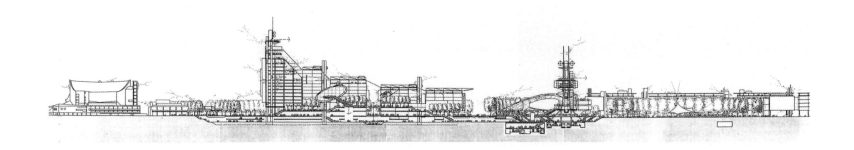

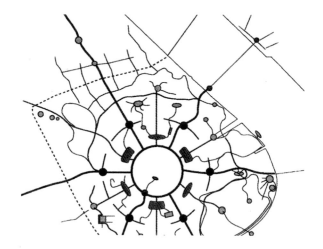

ratepayers to meet the bill. We show no inclination to try to follow in their footsteps, preferring instead to sit in a constantly cooling bath of the cosily familiar rather than face up to what is really happening to the urban environment. And that could be the reason that so little has come of Rogers' attempts to design on the scale of a city.

In London, his Thameside proposals seemed to belong more to the breathless world of the atomic-powered ocean liner, than the realm of achievable civic improvement, and the startling images of the partnership's urban schemes tended to draw attention away from his shrewdly civilised proposals to remove traffic congestion from the city centre, and to unite the north and south of the river into a whole. In Berlin, where Rogers began to work from the end of the 1980s, the difficulties of knitting together two halves of a city were even more pronounced. Divided into two unequal halves by twenty-nine miles of wall, it was rather less than the sum of its parts, adding up to nothing much more than two separate but physically contiguous backwaters, squashed uncomfortably close together. Now, united as the capital of eighty million Germans, it mounts a serious challenge to both London and Paris as Europe's leading metropolis after three decades of fossilisation. And the Rogers Partnership is still there, working with Renzo Piano and the consortium of developers who acquired the Potsdamer Platz just as the wall was coming down, with the intention of reconstructing it as a major new commercial heart of the city.

The site, flattened by damage from war-time bombing and Cold War free-fire zones, runs from the fragments of the baroque city of the east to the Kulturforum of Mies van der Rohe's Museum of Modern Art and Scharoun's concert hall in the west – modernist objects floating in fractured space. Rogers' strategy was to create a clear massing discipline, while giving a distinct identity to each site so that each consortium member could build structures that would be identifiably their own. The plan retained compositional control and established a set of urban design guidelines to achieve maximum environmental quality, integrate the development with its setting, and create the right skyline profiles, grain and scale. Rogers accepted that the Leipziger Platz should be reinstated to the original plan form and that historical building heights on this part of the site should be respected. 'The prospect and alignment of the link to Brandenburg Gate must be emphasised and we propose to recreate part of the Minstergarten. The traditional road pattern is maintained as it defines existing site boundaries, emphasises the historical axis and provides the outline of the public realm,' stated the partnership. Yet these rational proposals fell foul of Berlin politics, and the timidity of the city's senate. Like the primmer Victorians, they wanted a garden city, not a metropolis, a recreation of long-vanished baroque blocks.

But as it happens, Rogers was finally able to work within the context of a city whose future says much more about the city of tomorrow than either London or Berlin. At the

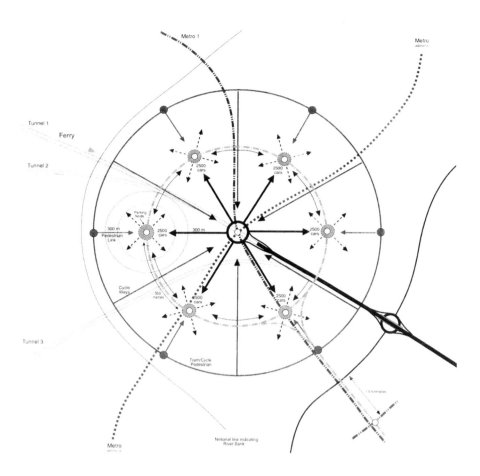

The relationship of a
great city to its riverfront
was as important to Rogers'
masterplan for a new
business district for Shanghai,
opposite and below left, as
it had been in the Royal
Academy study for London.
In diagrammatic form,
with circular rail loops for
transport, the project
deliberately echoed the
form of Ebenezer Howard's
Garden City, but the scale,
with its skyscrapers, and
its 500,000 inhabitants was
vastly different.

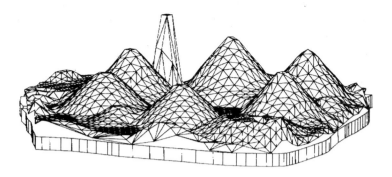

To accommodate the offices
and apartments needed by
Shanghai's mushrooming
economy, Lu Jia Zu – modelled
by computers, *above* –
would need to rise sixty floors
in some areas. The television
mast on the left-hand side
of the project, *opposite*, was
approved for the site before
Rogers became involved.

end of 1992, the mayor of Shanghai endorsed the Rogers Partnership's interpretations
of a development brief drawn up under the auspices of an international team from
Paris, with engineers and traffic planners from Ove Arup and researchers from the
Universities of London and Cambridge, as the basic for a masterplan to shape the
development of Lu Jia Zui, a 40 million square foot business centre for the city –
eight times the size of Canary Wharf in London.

Lu Jia Zui would be the focus of a modern new centre for the city, across the
sewage-choked, heavy metal-contaminated Huangpu River from the hallucinatory
skyline of the Bund, that remarkable slice of 1930s western urbanism marooned in
Asia. The Bund gave Shanghai a world famous skyline, but on a nineteenth-century
scale. Lu Jia Zui will relate to it, but it will be larger – on a scale appropriate to a city of
the twentieth-first century. A forest of sixty-storey skyscrapers, accommodating more
than 500,000 people would be grouped around a circular park, half a mile across, like
a collision between Regent's Park and Manhattan, sweeping away a suburb currently
occupied by two-storey courtyard houses. A series of boulevards would radiate out
from the centre of the development, which would be ringed by a circular light railway,
and linked to the rest of the city by new tunnels, bridges and two new metro lines.

Such a confrontation between present-day Shanghai with its seven million bicycles
and the city of tomorrow is too much for the squeamish to face up to. Yet the future
for Shanghai is never going to be picturesque and Dickensian, nor green-tiled, dragon-
roofed neo-Chinese. Instead it is a model of the urban future that has a real relevance
to the burgeoning cities of Asia, from Bangkok, which is building new suburbs to
house 250,000 people at a time, to Jakarta, a construction boom town. It is here
that a new model for the city is being created, although at the moment there is no
conceptual underpinning on offer other than unplanned Houston-style chaos, or
Third World shanty town squalor. Rogers' plan is a reminder that there are more
serious alternatives to the stage-sets of those who believe that the urban model
of Renaissance Europe still has some relevance to the post-industrial city, and goes
some way towards filling this gap.

'Of course, this plan is for China, but it is hard to say how Chinese it is,' says Rogers.
'If we were asked to design the same thing for Florida, there would be differences of
course – such as the climate, obviously, and the cultural preconceptions of the society
building it – but it is a modern city, and cities all over the world are shaped by the same
kind of pressures.'

Shanghai has always been China's most outward-looking city. Its most concentrated
previous period of growth came in the years after 1840, when the British fought the
Opium War to secure their trading rights with China. Most of its centre was built
between 1900 and 1935, when there were up to 60,000 westerners living there. By

the end of this century, China's present spurt of growth could give it the world's largest economy. In the ten years since China opened up to the outside world, the skylines of its big cities have been transformed by tawdry joint venture skyscrapers of the crudest kind. They are hardly preferable to the relics of Chairman Mao, who rebuilt the country on the basis of, as he put it, 'Economy, utility and, if possible, beauty'.

Rogers' plan is a high-minded attempt to create a mixed slice of the city that does not die at six in the evening, and is designed to minimise energy use and allow the maximum use of public transport. The strategy is to link the historic centre of Shanghai and the development zones on its outskirts with this new business district, making it an integral part of the city and not a separate, isolated town. The new settlement should have a design based on the street, and not create a field of independent island buildings, and it should be a pedestrian friendly city, and not designed only for the car. Also, says Rogers, it should mirror the curve of the river with what would be a dynamic plan rather than a static process. 'The world is increasingly aware of the damaging effects of uncontrolled or ill-planned development and growth. We aim to reduce energy consumption and the resultant pollution, which is why we have prepared a plan that is based on an integrated transportation strategy, where walking distances are reduced to a minimum, thus easing movement and reducing the dependence on car travel'.

Rogers has struggled to convince Shanghai that it should not build a single-function

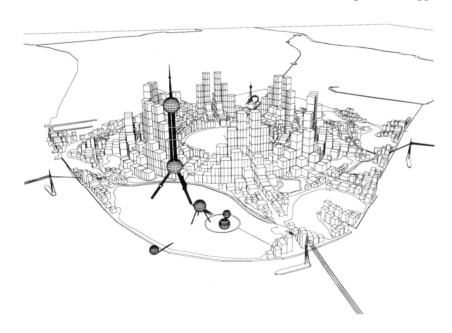

The cities of Asia are going through the kind of explosive growth that transformed London and Paris during the industrial revolution in the nineteenth century. If the millions of people pouring into them are to have any hope of a civilised future, they demand the boldness represented by the Shanghai project and the readiness to put industry to work that has been represented by Rogers' studies for low-cost prefabricated housing in Korea, *opposite*.

office desert. At the partnership's urging, the office content in the brief was reduced from eighty per cent to fifty per cent. The area is planned as six neighbourhoods, each no more than ten minutes walk from the next, and each one focused on one of six stations set 600 metres apart on the light railway that would orbit the development. There would be houses, hotels, shops, offices, museums and a conference centre, all of them disposed in a series of concentric rings of transport routes that echo the diagrams that Ebenezer Howard drew up for the Garden City at the end of the nineteenth century.

The most important feature of the transportation strategy within Lu Jia Zui is the light rail loop which defines the major spaces of the development area, and within which a maximum walking distance of 350 metres has been determined. This defines the maximum depth of the development zone from the light rail loop, while a network of centralised parking structures helps minimise vehicular movement. A circular feeder road along the inner edge of the development zone gives access to the parking structure, which allows 2,500 cars per neighbourhood, while vehicle access beyond these roads is restricted to taxis, bicycles, buses and delivery vehicles. A tram route around the outer edge of the development area, a pedestrian circle, a cycle circle, a tram circle and the light rail circle interlock with a series of radiating boulevards that describe the principle connections.

One of the guiding principles in the design was the determination to help Shanghai avoid mistakes made in the west. The project came at a time when the full extent of the shortcomings of the redevelopment of the Isle of Dogs in London's Docklands was becoming apparent. There, office buildings were built, catastrophically, before the transport infrastructure was even started. Not only was this an inadequate way to create a modern city, it put the economic future of the whole development in jeopardy. And unlike Rogers' plans for Shanghai, the Isle of Dogs had no range of activities to make it more than a nine-to-five office ghetto, and no connection with the surrounding communities. To Rogers, cities are vitally important for the continuation of civilised life. 'They provide the public space without which, in this age of telecommunications, public life will wither. The paradigm of public space is the city square or piazza, without which the city scarcely exists. City squares are special because their public function almost eclipses any other use they might have – people come to them principally to talk, demonstrate and celebrate, all of which are essentially public activities.' He draws a sharp distinction between this definition of public space and the reality of life in London: 'Its great squares, all doubling as traffic intersections, don't constitute squares at all.'

THE DOUBLE MEMBRANE DRIVES
THE NATURAL VENTILATION

AIR FROM THE ATRIUM VENTILATES
THE INNER OFFICES

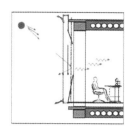

EXTERNAL LOUVRES WITHIN THE
MEMBRANE MINIMISE HEAT GAIN

DAYLIGHT SENSORS MONITOR AND
CONTROL USE OF ARTIFICIAL LIGHT

TEMPERED AIR IS SUPPLIED
DURING PEAK WINTER AND
SUMMER CONDITIONS

All offices are within 6m of an openable
window and are planned to provide
3m clear internal space for open plan use.

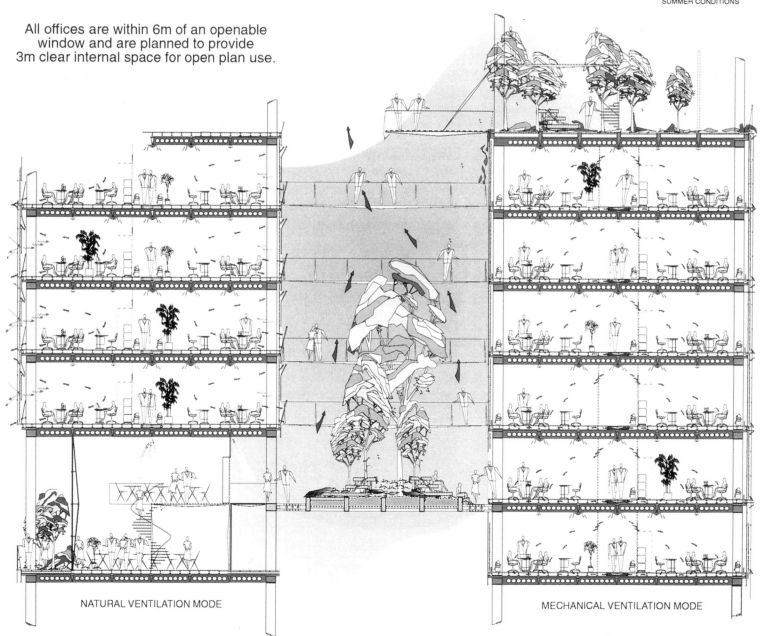

NATURAL VENTILATION MODE

MECHANICAL VENTILATION MODE

The role of technology in architecture is an ambiguous one. The infatuation of the pioneering modernists with the image of the machine age, at the expense of its substance, has resulted in a continuing mismatch between appearance and reality. Too many buildings, while attempting to posture as being just as technically advanced as the most innovative of industrially manufactured artefacts, have in fact failed to deliver the promised sophistication. Simply adopting a metal skin for a building, or aping the profile of an aircraft wing, does not make an earthbound structure acquire the characteristics of a jet liner. Furthermore, a coherent view of the energy performance of a building should be based on a sensitive response to climate and situation in such a way as to avoid the need for too much sophisticated technology. But there is a continuing strand in architecture in which design is based on a genuine concern with the substance of technical innovation, and with its application in appropriate ways. A diverse group of architects has a continuing interest in experimenting with new materials and techniques. Some of these are devised specifically for the building industry, others are co-opted from areas such as yacht building or the aircraft industry – activities which are, in fact, closer to building than they might at first sight appear. High-performance boats and aircraft are inevitably built in small numbers and rely on a high proportion of craft skills, rather than being churned out on genuine production lines. Contemporary British industry is at its best when it is manufacturing products in small batches to a high standard of quality. It is an updated version of traditional craftsmanship, based on the acceptance of technology and its possibilities. And it is an approach which seems to work well for racing cars and yachts, just as it once did for Savile Row tailors, sporting gun-makers, shoe-makers and motorcycle builders. It is only where genuine mass production is involved – in conventional cars, for example, and consumer electronics – that Britain comes unstuck.

Designed for a competition for a major site in Vienna, the twin tower project, *left*, was an attempt to make the maximum use of sun, daylight and natural forces to reduce the consumption of non-renewable energy in a high-rise building.

The atrium, rising the full height of the Vienna tower, *above*, would be used to draw in a controlled flow of external air, offering cool air from which internal offices would draw natural air circulation. Daylight would have been introduced through the atrium's gable ends, while a series of landscaped roof gardens would have been installed within the atrium.

These workshop industries, where high performance is at a premium, are frequently researching into new materials and methods which will save weight and increase strength, with the materials often having a seductive visual quality as well a technical rationale. The shackles and clips on which modern sailing depends, the exotic composites that are used to mould skis and ski boots, the lightweight honeycomb structures and high-performance glues used to build aircraft, all offer rich possibilities to architects with an eye for economy of means.

The Richard Rogers Partnership would certainly number itself among this group. It revels in the physical aspects of construction, not in the conventional building trades such as brick-laying and carpentry, but in the scope for inventiveness that comes from the well-equipped workshop, and a close relationship with a skilled and open-minded technician. Like Jean Prouvé, John Young, who has worked with Rogers since 1965, does not believe that design can be made in isolation from the workshop, nor does he care for the accidents and the improvisation of the building process. He aims for precision and clarity, and spends a long time drawing before building, designing out the surprises. It was this thoroughness that gave the Lloyd's building its remarkable physical presence, a quality which even those who have no sympathy for the building's architectural ambitions, such as Philip Johnson, admire. The practice is not overawed by the rhetoric of standardisation and the fetish for off-the-peg components that has overwhelmed a certain part of British architecture ever since the first pictures of the Eames house appeared in the architectural press. But while it enjoys the aesthetic potential of new materials, its interest is rooted not in technology for technology's sake but in a drive to use technology to provide elegant, economical solutions and for socially responsible ends. Architects, after all, are not entirely autonomous artists answerable only to their creative instincts. Their decisions and skills play a crucial role in environmental and social issues. The determinism of the 1960s – the idea that the shape of a room or the position of a window could modify people's behaviour – may have been misplaced and over-done, but it was always Rogers' ambition to use design to make the building process more pleasant for those actually engaged in it, and to reduce both the initial and the long-term costs of construction to society.

The years since the first oil shock of 1973 have been characterised by an increasing determination among all responsible architects to base their work on sounder ecological principles. In fact, this has always been an essential aspect of the architect's work – the issue of orientation has inevitably been concerned with the improvement of the thermal performance of the building. Siting a building to make the most of sunshine, views and breezes is one aspect of a passive energy management system. A good site gives a building some of its most vital qualities, as well as making energy sense too. The architects of Rogers' generation began to rediscover this approach a decade ago. Having once used energy to cancel out the effects of site and climate, they began to look again at the techniques that architecture had evolved over the centuries for dealing with climatic extremes: at the Arab tower houses that include a natural flue to circulate air; at the Moorish courtyards of Seville that condition air naturally. Energy-conscious buildings have to rely on a rather more substantial foundation of knowledge than a collection of visual mannerisms and philosophical prejudices. The counter-cultural slant to the ecology movement in the 1970s encouraged the assumption that technological responses to environmental issues were in themselves mistaken. In this context there was a tacit assumption that bamboo and methane and bicycle power were sounder, more politically correct propositions than the computerised monitoring of environmental control systems, even if the latter could actually do far more to cut down energy consumption. So-called 'Green' building was in danger of being reduced to a style, rather than representing a serious attempt to reduce society's consumption of scarce resources, and to maintain an equilibrium between man and the environment.

The equations are not always as transparent as the most simplistic interpretations would suggest. Compare the relative merits of using copper cables laid on the ocean bed over thousands of miles for telephone lines, in the approved early twentieth-century manner, with launching a single communications satellite of far greater capacity. The satellite might seem like the high-tech answer, yet it is conceivably much less profligate in its use of resources.

The Rogers office has devoted considerable time and thought to such issues. It has its preference for exact, precise materials such as glass and steel over stone, concrete and brick, which are less exact and more labour intensive. But it is well aware of the implications in energy terms of using glass walls. Therefore, although the Lloyd's building, for example, is extensively glazed, it is done in a way that minimises energy use. The glass, which is well insulated, and in some places treble-glazed, is specially formulated to reduce solar gain, while its dimpled surface is designed to give the façades a sparkle even on overcast days.

Considering architectural performance in this way means that technology is not a single equation that can be applied as a bolt-on extra, or an appendix to the design process. Rather it is an issue that plays an integral part in every aspect of design, from the largest scale of masterplanning in which mixed functions help to reduce the unnecessary use of the car, as does the proper integration of appropriate mass-transit systems, to the smallest, such as the provision of a sun-screen on an exposed south-facing façade. It can be the determining factor in shaping a building's form and orientation. For example, though deep plans may be more efficient in terms of reducing energy loss, shallow plans lessen dependence on artificial light and can be designed to avoid the need for air-conditioning. Opening a window is a more energy-efficient way to ventilate a building than supporting a plant room full of heat exchangers and chillers, all dependent on the use of fossil fuel energy. These are considerations that play a part in the selection of materials, not just sustainable timbers but also the exotic and possibly ozone-depleting gases used in air-conditioning and even in some fire-fighting systems.

Accommodating technology is also a vital part of planning a building to give it a satisfactory life in long-term use. The word flexibility is over-used and threadbare. But the speed with which so many things that initially seem like fixed landmarks in the modern landscape evaporate into irrelevance is remarkable. In the 1980s, the information technology revolution made the shallow plan, low ceiling-height office slabs of the 1960s and 1970s seem instantly obsolete. Many of them were duly demolished in haste to make way for deep-plan dealing room spaces with floors the size of football pitches, and increased floor-to-ceiling heights to accommodate the mass of ducts and cables needed to cope with two computer screens at every desk. Now these buildings are in turn looking over-specified as computer systems have continued to shrink in size and grow in power. It is the job of the architect to strike a judicious balance between present needs and future responsibilities .

The architect's role is seen by the partnership as crucial in developing a policy of sustainable development for society. In a typical city, the Rogers Partnership calculates, nearly half of all energy is consumed by the buildings – just five per cent of it through construction and the rest through lighting, heating and cooling. Industrial users in a typical city account for twenty-five per cent of the total energy consumption, while another twenty-five per cent is used by transport. The masterplan proposed by the partnership for the Parisian new town of Val d'Oise, a group of existing settlements

The Rogers masterplan for Val d'Oise on the outskirts of Paris, *below*, went several steps on from treating energy performance as a matter of individual buildings, and looked instead at the whole town from an energy point of view, from transport to orientation, and from materials to insulation.

and planned new development around Le Bourget Airport to the north of the French capital, set out to achieve a major reduction in energy consumption. It was a study with significant lessons for the shape of the modern city, and the partnership drew on it for its plans for Shanghai. The practice believed that it was vital to tackle the issue of energy at the level of infrastructure design, as well as that of individual buildings. They calculated that it would be possible to build the new Val d'Oise in such a way as to achieve energy savings of sixty per cent compared with a conventional modern development, provided that its form was determined by climatic considerations, rather than the requirements of the automobile. What they call 'a responsible energy strategy' depends on four key elements: better thermal insulation standards would be the most important single element, followed by the maximum use of natural ventilation. The balance of the savings would be made by making use of solar gain

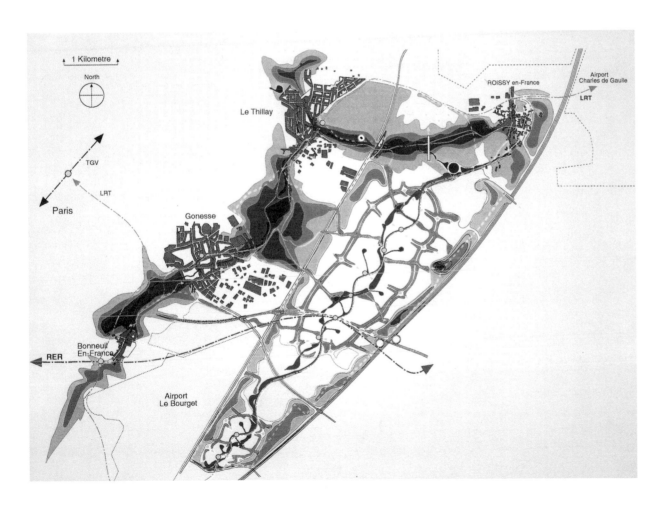

for water heating, and the installation of more efficient systems and management technology. But the strategy did not stop there. By incorporating natural ventilation and daylighting in factories, industry's use of energy could be halved. And the plan would have seen a huge reduction in the amount of energy being used for transport in Val d'Oise through the greater use of public transport, adopting integrated planning policies and more efficient rolling stock and motive power for a light rail rapid transit loop that would link the town with its neighbours.

Rogers' consultants calculated that if you took an infrastructure planned with efficient energy use in mind, and added to that the impact of using a combined heat and power system and renewable energy sources as well, then the net energy use could come down to just twelve per cent of that of a traditional town. It would mean a town geared not to the needs of the car, but one with a layout that responds to climate, sun, wind direction, views and topography. It would maximise the use of daylight, minimise the use of electricity for lighting and encourage a community-wide energy self-sufficiency strategy. Regarding the detailed design of individual buildings, one of the key projects in which the partnership evolved its approach to energy-efficient architecture was its submission in the invited competition for the Inland Revenue's new Nottingham building, a huge office complex under the shadow of Nottingham Castle, and a commission that was finally won by Michael Hopkins in 1991.

The role of design in energy-saving is now officially recognised. The EC directives

Journey times to the work places of Val d'Oise, *below*, would be kept to a minimum by mixing offices with residential accommodation and developing a network of canals.

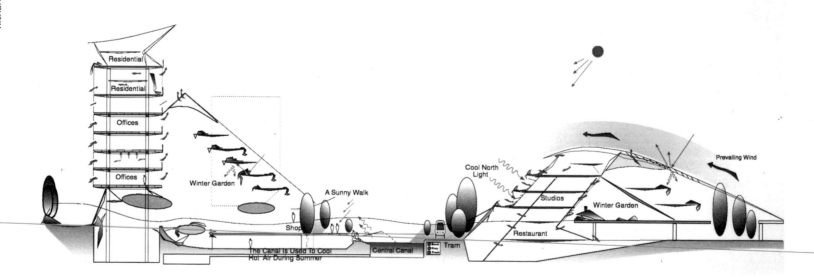

relating to the construction of major government buildings such as the Inland Revenue project now require that a full environmental impact analysis is to be carried out before construction starts. There are standard environmental specifications to cover the use of fluocarbons, the production of greenhouse gases, toxicity and the use of replenishable woods. These are now almost givens. The role of the creative architect is to put them to work with imagination. The brief from the Inland Revenue asked for 'offices fit for their purpose, and which provide value for money, and which are in sympathy with the environmental context, and enhance it'. In the partnership's view, that meant respecting views of Nottingham Castle, and reinforcing the landscape of the immediate environment, but it also meant an environmentally friendly building, a flexible workplace which could absorb growth and change, and a workplace with a sense of community. To this end, the building is orientated in such a way as to act as a buffer from the noise and the pollution from the railway line on the edge of the site, and to provide the largest possible landscaped open space facing on to the canal that forms one boundary. Its form provides shelter from prevailing winds, and protects its interior from unwelcome heat gain from the sun.

The view from the castle looking down over the Inland Revenue site was seen as particularly important. The sloping roof, with its part glass, part solid panels, was treated as the fifth elevation, set in densely landscaped grounds and free of the usual

The ground-hugging profile of the Inland Revenue building, *below*, would have encouraged natural ventilation, with orientation helping to reduce solar gain.

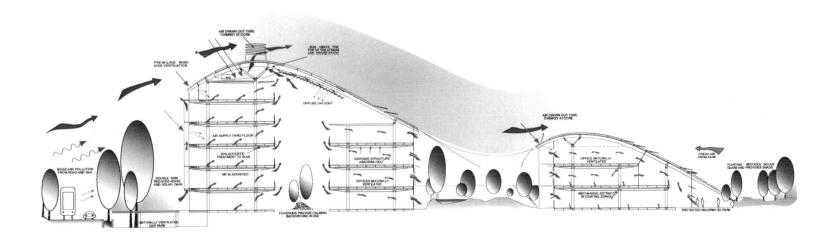

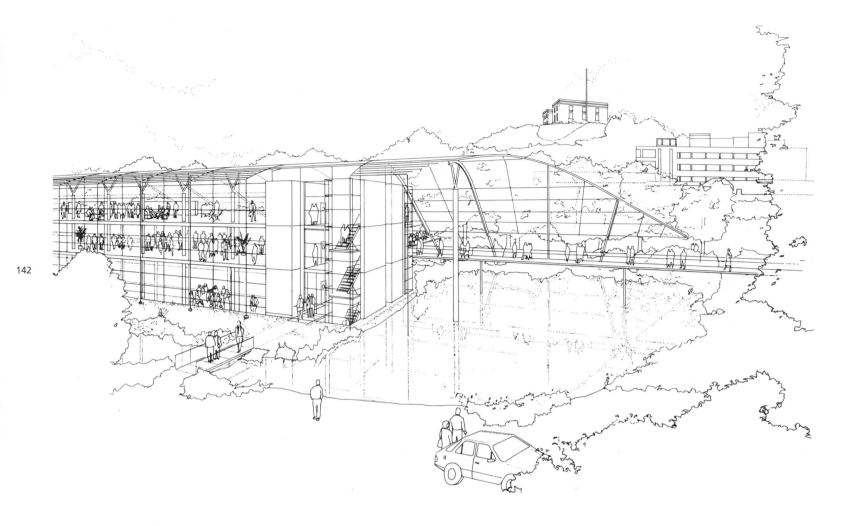

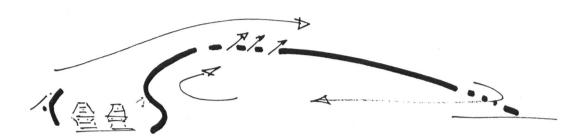

The decision to move large numbers of Inland Revenue civil servants out of London to a new building in Nottingham was accompanied by an architectural competition, eventually won by Michael Hopkins. The brief specified an environmentally-conscious approach to the design, which in Rogers' case was achieved through the use of passive environmental controls.

The Inland Revenue site in Nottingham is overlooked by the city's castle, which made the design of the roof particularly important. For Rogers it became a fifth elevation.

paraphernalia of mechanical servicing plants, ducting, cooling towers and all conventional office roof finishes. The absence of the unsightly trappings of a conventional air-conditioning installation would have been achieved by relying instead on passive environmental control, a mix-mode heating and cooling system which limits its major mechanical interventions to summer and winter peaks and troughs. In this way, while the building systems have the capacity to react mechanically when needed, normal operation is limited to the manipulation of existing external air to ensure the comfort of the workforce.

All the facades, except the southern side, which is a sealed double skin designed to deflect the noise and cut out pollution from the railway line, have opening windows. Computer modelling would have been used to identify any individual hot spots, to allow the architects to iron out problems before construction. It is true that the temperature variations in such a building are greater than those in conventionally air-conditioned buildings, but, as Rogers points out, this makes you more aware of the seasonal fluctuations, which is a benefit rather than a handicap. Low-energy building servicing systems rely on orientation to reduce unwanted heat gain and loss, and on tapping into free sources of energy and light. These sources of energy would have been utilised in varying densities to control internal thermal comfort in the Inland Revenue building.

Each floor would have contained a combined raised computer floor and plenum. During most of the year, most areas of the building rely on fresh air from open windows, but the southern offices, with the sealed skin, would draw on the plenum system for fresh air. During summer peak temperatures, some mechanical cooling would have been required, using heat exchange, with canal and ground water rather than by mechanical refrigeration plant. During the winter, all areas would have a

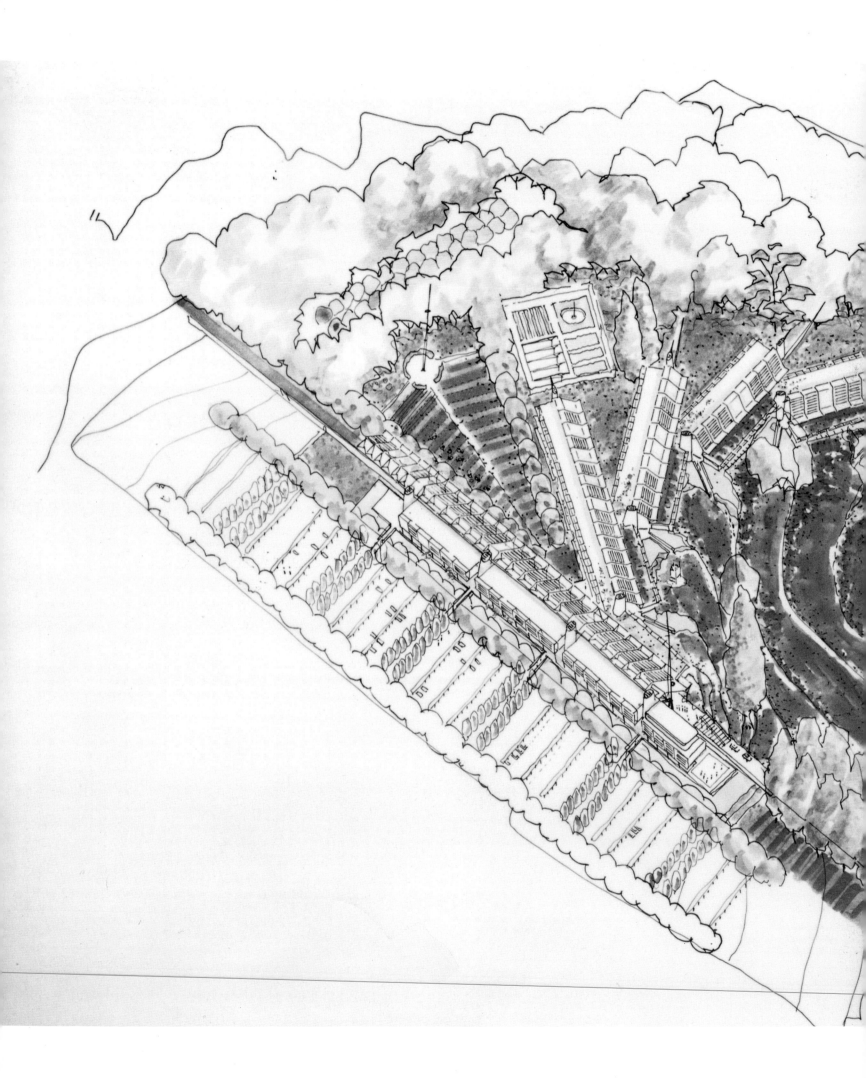

The partnership was successful in another competition to design the new home of Lloyd's Register of Shipping, *left*, completed in 1993. Here the setting was again an important factor, accounting for the low, site-hugging form of the building.

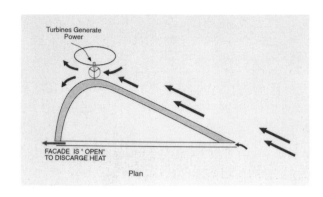

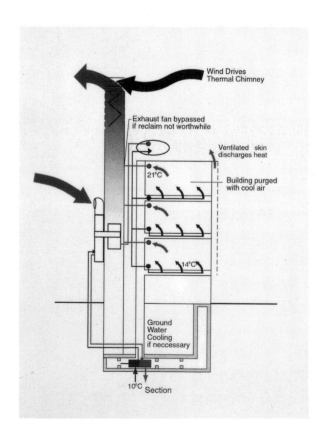

Developed with Arup engineers, the turbine tower, *above and right*, is a research project for a site in Tokyo's Tomigaya district. It explores ways of using the form of a building to generate power.

conditioned fresh air supply, heated by solar energy, and heat recovery. Finned tube heating would maintain comfort in the perimeter offices, and the system would be capable of being adapted to provide personal control and being automatically overidden in periods of high solar gain.

With its use of extensive landscaped interior atria, there would have been scope to use the ground water in the atrium pool to provide cooling during the summer peaks, while the cross-section of the building lent itself to the use of heat to drive stair air upwards, to create a stack effect for ventilation. During the summer nights, external air would have cooled the structural floor slabs to reduce the cooling load the following day, a process that would take place in reverse during the winter extremes.

In the partnership's competition-winning design for the Lloyd's Register of Shipping in Hampshire the design of internal and external spaces is also integrated to temper the working environment, thereby minimising the use of energy. But it is not just these relatively straightforward, low and discreet buildings that have been the focus for an energy-orientated approach to design. In Japan, the partnership's proposals for building a tall slender tower at Tomigaya, a triangular patch of ground close to Tokyo's Yoyogi Park, would actually use the building's form as a device to generate energy. With its blade and detached tower form, the structure would act as a wind turbine, accelerating wind speed across its surface, and capable of generating fifty-five kilowatts per hour, more than enough to service the building and to provide some power as well. The heavy concrete structure would be exposed to absorb heat and moderate the internal environment. The core is separated from the main building block and the building is smooth and shaped in such a way as to encourage the wind to pass through the gap between the building and the services tower to the north. It acts as a chimney under the influence of the sun and wind to extract used air. The northern façade is patterned with clear, diffuse and opaque panels to allow views and light, while providing insulation where needed. The southern façade, fully glazed at the client's request, has a variable shading system – tuned according to the time of day, the season and whether the sun is shining. The water pool around the deep basement is used for peak summer cooling and to warm cool air in winter, a total energy system in which each element is tuned to achieve low running costs.

Another example of the partnership tackling building types not conventionally regarded as susceptible to an energy-saving approach was the competition entry for a twin tower development in Vienna in 1993. All offices would have been within six metres of an openable window and were designed to be naturally ventilated and daylit for the majority of the year. For periods of prolonged cold or heat, each office has the option of utilising back-up mechanical heating or cooling. An external thermal flue ventilation system allows the towers, which are of course subjected to high wind

velocities, to be naturally ventilated. This comprises an outer layer of glass perforated top and bottom acting as a pressure-reducing valve, allowing offices to have opening windows on the internal skin. A blind system behind the outer skin allows precise and variable solar control. During the extremes of winter the building skin is sealed. Air is supplied by way of the raised floor plenum by compact floor-to-floor air-handling units. Triple-glazing and high insulating values would ensure minimal heating requirements. Again, during mid summer, the building can be sealed against hot air.

To Rogers such ambitious environmental systems are not a new departure in themselves, but simply represent the developments of the high insulation standards of the Zip-Up housing projects that he was working on in the 1960s. It is an integral part of his architectural approach. They are not an end in themselves, or an after-thought, but provide an essential starting point for the design of responsible buildings. This has nothing to do with stylistic mannerisms, but is work based on attitudes and philosophies that take contemporary architecture in important new directions.

The partnership won an international architectural competition to design a new complex of courtrooms for Bordeaux, *opposite*, a design which involved a sensitive historic site and a commitment to energy-saving. Rogers employed heat exchanges, natural ventilation and a careful consideration of orientation to fulfil the brief.

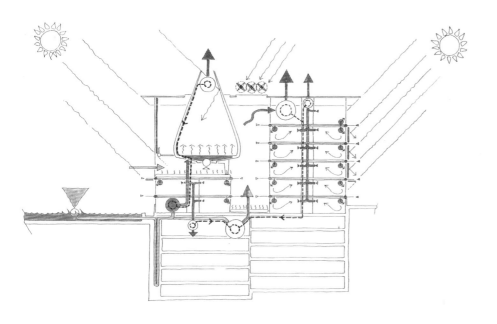

Buildings and projects

Key
Buildings under construction or completed
Projects

Team 4

1963	Pill Creek Retreat, Feock, Cornwall
1964	*Waterfront Housing, Pill Creek, Feock, Cornwall*
1965	*Wates Housing, Coulsdon, Surrey*
1966	Jaffe House, Radlett, Hertfordshire. House at Creek Vean, Feock, Cornwall
1967	Three houses , Murray Mews, London
	Electronics Factory for Reliance Controls, Swindon (demolished)

Richard + Su Rogers

1967- 68	Spender House, Ulting, Essex
1968-1971	*Zip-Up House 1 & 2*
1968-1969	House for Richard Rogers' parents, Wimbledon, London
1969-1971	Office and studios for Design Research Unit, Aybrook Street, London
1969-70	Factory for Universal Oil Products, Phase 1, Ashford, Kent

Piano + Rogers

1971-1977	Centre Pompidou, Paris
1971	Service module for ARAM, temporary field hospital
1971-1977	Institut de Recherche et Co-ordination Accoustique/Musique, Paris
1972-1973	Offices and factory for B+B, Italia, Como
1973	*Park Road Development, St John's Wood, London*
1973-1974	Factory for Universal Oil Products, Phase 2, Tadworth, Surrey
1974-1976	Furniture for the Pompidou Centre, Paris
1974	*Research Laboratory, East Anglia*
1975	Apartment in Place des Vosges, Paris
1975-1983	Patscentre Phases 1 & 2, Melbourn, Cambridgeshire
1977	*Millbank Riverside Housing, Pimlico, London*
	Fleet Air Arm Museum, Yeovilton, Somerset

Richard Rogers Partnership

1978	Elias House, Long Island, New York
	Autonomous House, Aspen, Colorado
	Furniture for Knoll International
	Lloyd's of London Headquarters, City of London (completed 1986)
1979	Napp Laboratories, Cambridge
	Fleetguard Centre, Quimper, Brittany (completed 1983)
	Coin Street Development, London
1981	Free Trade Wharf Development, London
1982	Inmos Microprocessor Factory, Newport, Gwent
	PA Technology Laboratory, Princeton, New Jersey (completed 1985)
	National Gallery Extension, London,
1983	Development for banks of the River Arno, Florence
	Whittington Avenue offices, City of London
1984	Industrial Units Maidenhead, Berkshire (completed 1985)
	Thames Wharf Studios Complex, Hammersmith, London (completed 1985)
	North Park Shopping Centre, Houston, Texas
	First United Methodist Church, Seattle, Washington
	Royal Docks Strategic Plan, Docklands, London
1985	Linn Products Factory, Glasgow (completed 1987)
	Billingsgate Securities Market, City of London (completed 1988)
	Offices at 375 Hudson Street, New York
1986	H. H. Pegg, Thames Wharf, Rainville Road, London
	Wellcome Foundation Headquarters,
	Bracken House, City of London, London
	London As It Could Be, Exhibition, Royal Academy of Arts, London
	Floating Restaurant, South Bank, River Thames, London

Centre Commercial Forum d'Epone, Epone, France
Vom Landmark Buildings, Royal Victoria Dock, London
Usines Center, Commercial Centre, St Herblain, Nantes, France
Brunswick Wharf, Docklands, London
Royal Albert Dock Development, Docklands, London

1987

Surrey Quays, Surrey Docks, Canada Water, London
Royal Avenue House, London
Pump House, Royal Victoria Docks, London
Blackwall Yard Phase 1, Docklands, London (completed 1989)
Stag Development, Competition, Victoria, London
Paternoster Square, St Paul's, City of London
Massy Autosalon, Massy, France
Novoli Project, Florence
Iikura Building, Tokyo
Kabuki-cho Building, Tokyo (completed 1993)

1988

Pont d'Austerlitz, Paris
GRC Headquarters 1 & 2, Lyons
Berlin Modell Industriekultur, Berlin, Germany
Alcazar development, Marseilles

1989

Jimbocho Kanda, Tokyo
Scientific Generics, Cambridge
New Terminal at Marseille Airport (completed 1992)
Canal +, Paris
Farnborough Airport, Farnborough
Lyon Satolas Competition, Lyons
Canary Wharf Tower, London
Reuter's Recreation Facility, Docklands, London (completed 1991)
European Court of Human Rights, Strasbourg (completed 1994)
Chiswick Park Area 2, London
Terminal 5 Heathrow Airport, London (completion 2002)

1990

Ningyo-cho, Tokyo
Tokyo Forum Competition, Tokyo
Tomigaya Exhibition Building, Tokyo
Shinkawa, Tokyo
Christopher Columbus Centre, Baltimore, Maryland
Futurum Diner
Office Development, Grosvenor Road, London
Masterplan, Bussy St George, Marne La Vallée, France
Tour des Medias, Eurallile, Lille
Michael Elias House, California
Offices for Stockley Park, West London
Daiwa Europe House, London Wall, City of London
Masterplan, King's Dock, Liverpool
Port Aupec, Paris
Channel 4 Headquarters, London (completed 1994)
Masterplan, Dunkirk Neptune, Dunkirk
Zoofenster Building, Berlin
Neue Messe, Leipzig

1991

John Young's Apartment, Thames Reach, London
Roppongi Studio, Tokyo
Roger's Weekend House
Masterplan, Nice, La Plaine 2, Nice
Industrialised Housing System, Korea
Masterplan, Potsdamer/Leipziger Platz, Berlin

1992	Liverpool Arena, King's Dock, Liverpool
	Turbine Tower Research Project, Tokyo
	Headquarters for Inland Revenue, Nottingham
	Headquarters for SmithKline Beecham, London
	Headquarters for Süddeutsche Zeitung, Munich
	Masterplan for Schulteiss Brewery, Spandau, Berlin
	Daimler Benz Competition, Potsdamer Platz, Berlin
	Gallus Park, Frankfurt Am Main
	Masterplan, Val d'Oise, Roissy, Paris
	Brno Technology Park, Czech Republic
	Takizawa Bridge, Japan
	Masterplan, Shanghai Lu Jia zui, Shanghai
	Europier, Heathrow Airport, London
	Terminal 1 Expansion, Heathrow Airport London (completed 1994)
1993	Daimler Benz Offices, Berlin
	Headquarters for Lloyd's Register Of Shipping, Liphook, Hampshire
	Bordeaux Judiciare, Bordeaux
	Masterplan, Dortmund
	Berlin Underground, Berlin
	Masterplan, Treptow, Berlin
	Twin Towers, Vienna

Index